Anonymous

**Sybelle**

And Other Poems

Anonymous

**Sybelle**
*And Other Poems*

ISBN/EAN: 9783744711234

Printed in Europe, USA, Canada, Australia, Japan

Cover: Foto ©Thomas Meinert / pixelio.de

More available books at **www.hansebooks.com**

# POEMS.

# SYBELLE

AND

## OTHER POEMS.

By L.

بها

NEW YORK:

*Carleton, Publisher,* 1 3 0 *Grand St.*

(LATE RUDD & CARLETON.)

M DCCC LXII.

# Dedication.

---

## To HENRY W. LONGFELLOW, Esq.:

EVEN as a child with tender reverence brings
From its small store some treasured offerings,
Which, trifles though they be, yet serve to prove
To those more wise its confidence and love,
So at thy feet, O Bard of high renown,
I trusting lay my humble offering down,
Not as all worthy thus to boldly claim
The well-prized favor of thy glance — Thy fame
Checks the fond hope my untaught lips would frame;
Yet nature tells me he who tunes his lyre
So oft in woman's praise; who wakes such fire
Of pure and tender love as Preciosa owns;
Who walks unwearied through life's changeful zones
Still cheered and guided by the flame divine
That lures the hopeful, sad Evangeline;
Who, waiving custom's laws, makes nature speak
On fair Priscilla's lip and changing cheek;
Who, more than all, paints with a master's hand
The dark-browed children of our western land,
Who moves all hearts, as Hiawatha's moved,
To the true, tender woman whom he loved,
Then throws o'er all the warrior's grief and gloom,

viii CONTENTS.

# SYBELLE.

# SYBELLE.

## PART I.

IN FOREST depths a rose is springing,
In thickets lone a thrush is singing,
A traveler listens to the song,
Kisses the rose, and wonders long
That such sweet bloom and minstrelsy
In lonely woodland wilds should be.
Softly he kneels, and soft has pressed
The wild rose to his lips, his breast,
And smiled to see the wondrous glow
His kisses on the flower bestow.
He speaks some tender passing word—
The thrush has in the thicket heard;
Its plaintive, spring-born lays are stilled,
By some strange power its breast is thrilled,
And lo! the wildwood depths along,
Rolls the full summer tide of song.
O, will the charméd wanderer stay,
To bless the rose, inspire the lay,
Through all life's blissful summer day,
But asking that when life has fled,

Those blushing leaves be o'er him shed,
And that the parting song may bear
His rapt soul to Elysium fair?
Or will one passing hour like this,
Endow him with such wealth of bliss
He can all else forego, and brave
As men are, climb to make his grave
Among the glaciers flashing cold,
And rocks o'erlying gleams of gold,
High on life's barren summit, where
Nor song nor summer roses are?
And in the vale, if he should go,
Would still the rose in beauty blow?
Would still the song so joyous flow?
Go down at twilight in the vale,
And ask them both to tell the tale,
For none beside the flower and bird
Those words and kisses felt or heard.

The summer eve is hushed and calm,
The airs of June are breathing balm
From wild flowers waiting for the dew;
The green leaves take a darker hue,
Save where the slanting sunset ray
Yet lingers on each westering spray,
Till rose-bloom tinged with blended gold,
Seems trembling in each emerald fold.
As some fond lover seeks to grasp
Her hand whose form he may not clasp,
Caress it o'er and o'er again,
Glad to prolong the parting pain,
Dreading the last reluctant kiss

That seals at once his doom and bliss —
So fond, so lingeringly the light
Plays round the greenwood leaves to-night,
So warmly passionate the glow
That trembles through the branches low,
And falls on every quivering leaf—
A passing glory, bright as brief.

By soft, low banks of green caressed,
The valley stream smiles in its rest;
Such murmuring rest, such dimpling gleams
Of smiles as bless a maiden's dreams,
When arrowy shafts of love-light part
The shades of doubt that cloud her heart,
As slanting rays of sunlight quiver
Through all the trees that shade the river,
And fall, so blessing and so blest,
Upon its trembling, happy breast.

Sybelle, with face as fair and calm
As this sweet hour of bloom and balm,
But form as still, and seeming cold,
As though she were not mortal mold,
Waits by the river's side to-night:
Around her falls the golden light;
Now on the green turf where she stands,
Now on her closely folded hands
The glory rests; unconscious still,
The slight form gives no answering thrill,
Though upward blushing from her lips
The shade that marks the day's eclipse,
Goes deepening, warming in its hue,

Above her cheeks, her eyes of blue,
Above her forehead calm and fair,
Till like a halo round her hair
It flushes, pales, then fades in air.

What wondrous spell, what wizard glance
Has bound her in that dreamy trance?
'Tis not indifference, not surprise,
That fixes thus her steady eyes
With that strange look of vacancy,
That seeing all seems naught to see.
All sights and sounds of beauty here,
That meet her eye or charm her ear,
Have to each sense familiar grown
As though her life were nature's own,
And she a leaf, a flower, a bird,
By all their sweet emotions stirred,
Bloomed when they bloomed, sung when they sung,
Or in enchanted silence hung,
While summer sunlight round her played,
And summer winds their music made.
These are the haunts, where, when a child,
She found such inspiration wild
In all surrounding sympathies,
The changeful stream, the murmuring trees,
The blossoms on the hillside dying,
Or tempests through the dark sky flying,
As wakened in her youthful breast
Ambition's dreams, its strange unrest.
Vague dreams they were, for that young face,
That form so full of girlish grace,
The pure soul looking wistful through

# SYBELLE.

Those deep and tender eyes of blue,
Knew naught of fame save that the word
On many a careless tongue was heard;
And naught of life, unless it meant
Some change of outward element,
Such as the varying seasons made
When round her childish years they played,
When winter melting into spring
Would to her path fresh roses bring,
And summer's deepening blooms bestow
On cheek and lip a warmer glow,
Or autumns softly shadow down
Their brown leaves on her tresses brown.
Beloved and loving, her young years
Scarce found a place for grief or tears.
Yet, was the soul within content
That thus the summers came and went,
And found and left her like the flowers
That blossomed in her wildwood bowers,
Only a rose, or if a bird,
Still one whose songs were all unheard?

Content! Yes, as the lightnings are
That play around yon cloudy bar
Low lying in the southern skies,
So faintly tinged with sunset dyes.
Sybelle is gazing on it now,
A kindred light burns on her brow,
A bright flush tints her cheek of snow:
"I see it all," she murmurs low;
"I am the cloud; these wild desires
For name and fame, are lightning fires,

That burn and flash, and flash and burn,
And on themselves in vengeance turn,
That in their isolation driven
They touch not earth, they reach not heaven.
God's pity for the helpless cloud!
It fails and fades, a cold gray shroud,
From whose thin folds no blessed rain
Shall ever reach the thirsty plain.
With lightnings breathing quick and warm
Through all its elements of storm,
Alone, it faints, it fades from sight,
In' silence in the silent night.
It may be well. It may be, too,
That Raimond's cruel words were true;
That all the hopes within me born,
Like gossamers of summer morn,
With flaunting breadth of jewelled rim,
Would in the world's broad light grow dim,
And long ere noon their death doom meet,
From eager hands and trampling feet
Intent but on the ripened wheat.
The world, he says, has little need
Of blossoms culled from bank and mead;
Out of its young romancings grown,
Aside its dew-sprent sandals thrown,
It storms abroad in active strife,
Full of such earnestness of life,
That only high, heart moving songs,
Of love, and truth, and clashing wrongs
And rights, its stern, strong heart can move.
O, what is life? and what is love?
What is the world? and what am I?

Too feeble from this thrall to fly,
Too strong to be content and tame,
Must I still, like yon lightning flame,
Turn on myself?   O passing breeze,
Bring down some answer from the trees!
O sweet June roses, buds that shiver
In these light winds, beloved river,
And tender stems of grass that quiver
Where e'er I tread!   O forest birds
That sing to me in no vain words!
O many fashioned poet leaves,
Along whose lines the night wind weaves
Sublimest harmonies!   O light
Of this sweet eve!   O holy night,
That praiseth God with starry speech!
Have I learned so much that ye teach,
Lived with, loved, worshiped ye so long,
That my soul seems yourselves in song,
Yet knows not life, nor love, nor truth,
Such as give song immortal youth,
And to all time a deathless name
Linked with high thoughts, themselves their fame?
I thought I lived; he calls it dreaming:
Here then forever ends this seeming.
I waken now.   Waft back, O breeze,
Farewells to blossoms, birds and trees;
Life needs them not, and I no more
Bend in sweet worship as before,
At your pure altars.   I must learn
What life is; with high purpose turn
To other teachers, even to him
At whose light words my hopes grew dim.

The hand that laid these idols low,
Shall others in their place bestow.
The lip that smiled its pitying praise,
And called my offerings girlish lays,
Pretty and tender, yet shall give
The homage that to win I live!
O he would have a lightning flash
In every word, a thunder crash
In every line, and tempests hurled
Through each fair page to please the world!
Well, will he but the lesson teach,
My mind can grasp all his can reach:
Come, life!"
           Lo, echoing to the word,
Along the valley path is heard
A firm, light step.   It sounds so near,
The maiden starts as if in fear.


   " Sybelle!"


           The voice was soft and low,
Paled on her cheek the angry glow,
And such a bright and flitting smile
As sunset gave the leaves the while,
Touched the red lips, but quickly died,
And left the place to scornful pride.
She scorned herself that self-betrayed
So bare her inmost soul was laid
Even to the flowers; and what if he,
Half-feared, half-reverenced, could it be
That Raimond, idly dreaming near,
Had chanced her wild, strange words to hear?

And if he had, she thought, was pride
E'er yet in woman's need denied?
Alas, it sadly fails her now;
The blood flies burning to her brow,
She speaks his name, but vainly tries
To raise to his her drooping eyes,
Then murmurs, less in pride than guilt,
" Reproach and censure if thou wilt."


   He read her speaking face too well.
He took her hand :
                " Fair child, Sybelle,
No censure, no reproachful word
For you can from my lips be heard,
Even might I venture now to guess
What caused this passionate distress.
Did some strange vision come to you?
I have been watching visions too.
See where I sat, far up between
The trees that skirt the hillside green;
A soft, low, mossy mound is there,
Fringed round with ferns and blossoms fair,
And fitter for a fairy's throne
Than for these lengthened limbs I own.
Yet what I could of kingly grace
I summoned to adorn the place,
And sat, a king o'er such a land
As ne'er was won by warrior brand.
Long gazing at the golden fall
Of glory down heaven's western wall,
I saw, or fancied that I saw,
An angel hand the curtain draw :

An angel form came softly through;
It did not fly, for much like you,
No wings upon its shoulders grew!
Down toward a bright, celestial stream
It moved, as you move when you dream,
In maiden pride, with charm so sweet
As makes all other charms complete,
The outward motion but revealing
The inward strength and grace of feeling.
So moved the angel, and her eyes
Were looking toward the southern skies;
A soft, blue drapery round her fell,
Such as you wear to-night, Sybelle.
I know not how, perhaps I dreamed,
But as I gazed, the vision seemed
Most like to you; and then I thought,
By some romantic fancy caught,
Your steps in dangerous nearness strayed
To where the treacherous river played;
And, hero-like, I ran to save
A heroine from a watery grave!
Now, though the race be all in vain,
A hero should some guerdon gain,
Slight though it be; then come, Sybelle,
Soon fall the dews in this low dell,
While fair along yon wooded height
Yet lies the sunset's yellow light.
Come where the winding pathway trails
Its truant course through dainty vales,
Creeping and idling as it goes,
By mossy mounds and blooms of rose,
Yet upward still in its sweet way,

From twilights dim to where the day
Shines clear along the broad highway.
Idling like it shall be our walk,
And pleasant as its way our talk.

" I wonder much, Sybelle, of late,
What moody spirits round you wait.
Where are the fluttering, airy things
That fanned you with their gauzy wings;
That fed you nectar, kept you singing,
In strains like fairy music ringing —
That in your path their rose leaves flung,
And all around you rainbows hung?
You smile, but still your song, or lute,
To speak in poet phrase, is mute;
Your brow looks cramped as if in pain.
What goblin scared your fairy train,
Swept the sweet rose leaves from your path,
And stole your rainbows in his wrath?
I would I knew his name, Sybelle;
As my reward I pray you tell
What looks he like, what name he bears,
And where and how he spread the snares
To do such cruel, ruthless wrong,
As capture all your birds of song !
Sometimes you seem all lonely straying
To mournful marches round you playing,
And then all strength and fire and scorn,
As though you were a comet born,
And cared not where the planets went
So you flashed through the firmament.
This is not right, this is not life,

Come, tell me why this mental strife;
The dreary wilderness disclose
Where you are suffering thus; who knows!
Your life a Marah's stream may be,
The prophet I to find the tree
Whose healing balm can sweetness give,
And bid the wanderer drink and live."

Half gay, yet tender and sincere,
The words fell soothing on her ear,
Though well through all that playful art
She feared he read her inmost heart.
Nor could his tenderness subdue
The rebel fires upflashing through
The quick eyes lifted to his own,
And trembling in her eager tone.

"O might I only find the stream,
   No matter what its bitterness,
One deep, long draught would sweeter seem,
   Than all these years of nothingness!"

"Sybelle, life's stream is flowing here,
Even at your feet, so calm and clear,
So pure and sweet; why should you shrink
From its unsullied depths to drink?
Why turn toward stormier waves your eye,
While these untasted pass you by?"

"I must have more of life," she said;
   "I cannot breathe in this dull round;
Too low this sky droops overhead,
   And by this close horizon bound

All thought grows narrow, cramped, and tame,
Years pass, and others come the same;
Changeless in change they come and go,
And I but watch their ebb and flow.
My pale pink roses bloom and fade,
My timid violets haunt the shade,
My sunflowers, rimmed and rayed with gold,
Stand in their summer worship bold,
With just as much of life as I
Beneath this spot of summer sky."


" Yet you seemed happy when I came,
    Scarce one brief year ago, Sybelle;
Ah! now I guess the goblin's name,
  .  Whose presence broke your fairy spell.
O, he shall penance do more dire
Than quenching thirst with draughts of fire !
Was it my hand unstrung your lyre,
Sybelle ?"
                    So sudden changed his tone,
    The maiden started from his side;
His searching glances met her own,
    And heart to questioning heart replied.
From her proud, tender eyes the ray
Showed that ambition held its sway
O'er every passion of her breast,
Though scarce her woman's pride repressed
The tears at what those eyes confessed.
That instant, mute appeal for aid
His instant answering glance repaid,
From calm, clear eyes that said so well,·
You cannot ask in vain, Sybelle.

Slow, by the broad highway they pass,
Slow o'er the clover-sprinkled grass,
Down the long lane where sunset throws
Its last ray on the maple rows,
And pause where climbing roses twine
With clusters of the dark musk vine
Around the cottage porch, and fall
A robe of beauty o'er its wall.
Along the months so quickly fled
Have Raimond's hurried glances sped,
Recalling how, when first a guest
In this green valley of the west,
Brain-weary, worn with toil he sought
Forgetfulness of life, of thought,
And calm repose to cool the flame
Of fever burning through his frame,
He listened to Sybelle's sweet lay;
How pleased he read the artless play
Of her pure thoughts, caught from the breeze,
The birds, brooks, flowers and forest trees,
Through which her soul breathed all the grace
That nature gave her form and face;
Recalling too the proud surprise
That flashed light from her happy eyes,
When he had wondered why so long
Had been unheard her voice of song;
And then the still, sad, thoughtful air
With which she nerved herself to bear
All he had said the world would claim
From those who dared to ask for fame;
Her changed and wayward moods, and now,
The pleading eyes, the sweet, fair brow,

That looked so full of thought and pain,
So weary of its troubled brain;
The strangely passionate words that sprung
So oft, so eager from her tongue —
Yes, that brief, backward glance revealed
All·that Sybelle's proud heart concealed.
He saw her motives high and pure;
Though doubtful yet, and half obscure
Within his brain the question seemed,
Whether she waked or wildly dreamed.

" I almost grieve," he said, " Sybelle,
That e'er my darkening shadow fell,
So like a fated, restless wraith,
Across your quiet woodland path.
Not for myself — no, heaven knows
I never found a fairer rose,
Or music heard more pure and sweet
Than that which charms this lone retreat,
And holds me here, a willing guest;
And I, Sybelle, were doubly blest,
If aught I bring of worldly store,
Could add to your unstudied lore
One worthy element or thought
By that strange world's experience taught.
I would atone, if thus I might,
   For words in seeming harshness spoken,
Though never yet came day's fair light
   Till morning clouds and dreams were broken.)
Still, haply might the woodland stream
Choose in its twilight haunts to dream,
And rather watch the pale stars shine,

2

Than yield to guidance rude as mine,
To lead it where, with burning ray,
The sun pours down the perfect day.
You sigh, and turn your weary eyes,
As if afar, in foreign skies
Alone that longed-for day might be,
With years between its light and thee.
So heard I sighing, yester-morn,
The hillside brook beneath the thorn.
Thou knowest, Sybelle, what blushing ranks
Of roses bend along its banks;
I think they grow so very fair
For love of her who placed them there.
But yester-morn the wind shook down
The hawthorn's snowy garland crown;
And the meek roses, bending lower,
Ripe to the crimson-tinted core,
Dropped all their incense-breathing bloom,
Shrouding the stream in such sweet gloom,
It saw no heaven above it shine,
And pined as now I heard you pine —
When will the perfect day be mine?
Your life has been a low sweet psalm,
A woodland streamlet, clear and calm,
In happy tones its music blending
With bloom of flowers its banks o'erbending,
Yet ever deeper, stronger growing
From wayside fountains to it flowing,
And pressing like a human soul
Unconscious toward its destined goal,
Seeking by ways it might not know
The sea where life's deep waters flow.

"You sigh for fame.   O forest child,
Though o'er your birth the muses smiled,
Though step by step in childhood's hours
They led you through enchanted bowers,
Though round your maiden brow were wreathed
Their crowns, and on your lips were breathed
Their inspirations pure and high,
All these are still but prophecy,
Not deeds, that give you right to claim
That proud reward the world calls fame.
Ah, little cares that world to know
What time your wildwood roses blow;
How dimpling flows your forest stream,
Or how in twilight bowers you dream,
Tranced by the blended harmonies
Of summer leaves and sunset skies.
It would have thoughts born of the strife,
The conflicts of your hidden life,
Great truths from nature, and, as meet
From woman's hand, inwoven sweet
With tender human sympathies —
Love, grief, and joy; such themes as these
Reach its great heart, if from your own
Springs the key note, the moving tone,
The spark magnetic that alone
Touches all natures, and can thrill
The world obedient to one will.
O never poet's subtlest art
    Could weave you laurels from the air;
Go down into your woman's heart,
    And find your own crown jewels there!
Turn from the flowery, dim ideal,

And live and sing the present real.
Your own still life upon you palls —
Look out beyond your garden walls;
No close horizon's bound is there,
Nor low-drooped skies nor stagnant air.
The West! to me the very name
Sends blood new bounding through the frame.
In wilds like these, if e'er on earth,
Might giants claim immortal birth.
True life is here, and brave and strong,
Is working out a nation's song,
As foot by foot it marks the lines
From tropic plains to arctic pines,
And stanza after stanza sweeps
From prairie bounds to mountain steeps,
The golden chorus ringing o'er
The broad, fair land from shore to shore.
Thought grows not tame in life like this.
Nor were those years of nothingness
That round your young, pure being threw
Their bloom and shine, and sweet life dew;
Their springtime sunlights soft and dear,
Their autumn shadows chill and drear,
The splendors of their summer bloom,
Their winter nights of storm and gloom,
All were to you as suns, and showers,
And winds, and dews are to your flowers;
All molding you as they are molded,
When in the silent seed enfolded,
In perfect form embalmed they lie,
A slow unfolding mystery.
Nor breath of wind, nor fall of rain,
Nor dews nor sunlit skies were vain.

"Still in your eager, asking eyes
And on your lip unanswered lies
Your heart's great question.  Ah, Sybelle,
Words are of little worth to tell
What life is.  Life alone can give
Your answer — such as they must live
Who dare its doubtful strife to meet
    Matched hand to hand and soul to soul,
Nor dream of rest, nor know defeat
    Though baffled oft; but to the goal
For gain or fame, for good or ill,
Wage the stern war with tireless will;
Some grasping pleasure as they go,
But crowning victory with their woe;
Some worn and weary, conquering all,
And some the strongest, first to fall.
It is of that fierce warring world,
Of life in seeming chaos hurled,
Of mind to clashing mind opposed,
Of fates in life-long contest closed,
Of thought and passion, soul and sense —
The realm of mind's omnipotence,
That you are thirsting thus to know;
I read it in your cheek's bright glow,
I see your small hand closer clasped
As if some weapon it had grasped,
And dark flames kindling in your eyes
Uplifted toward the twilight skies,
Where neither sky nor stars you see,
But far and dim, like prophecy,
That distant world whose murmur comes
To you like beat of rallying drums

To armed and eager ranks, who wait
The signal note to seize their fate.

"Sybelle, you know how worn and pale,
And weary, to your quiet vale
For rest I came; how like a child
I wandered in these forests wild,
Pleased as a child whole summer days
To drown in that sweet, dreamy haze,
Made up of blossom-scents and song
Of birds and bees and sounds that throng
All fresh green summer woods; and how
When brown nuts ripened on the bough,
Boy-like I grew with growing health,
And reveled in the autumn wealth
Of forest fruits and painted leaves;
    Or helped the fallow fields to sow,
Or climbed the stacks to toss the sheaves
    Into the thresher's jaws below;
Or with the merry husking band,
In mimic contest, hand to hand
With practiced men my strength I plied,
Or at the plow my sinews tried;
Then vied with boys in winter sports
Of skating feats and snow-built forts;
Or with mute flocks and cattle sought
Companionship absolved from thought;
How to the slow-awakening spring
I lent my awkward aid, to bring
Your garden walks and beds and blooms
Out of their shroud of winter glooms;
Or with the planter's pouch and hoe

Traced o'er the fields the furrowed row,
Or sought for friends among the broods
Of birds that haunt your pleasant woods,
Or squirrels chattering through the glen —
All, anything but books and men
I welcomed; and not all in vain,
To nerves unstrung, exhausted brain,
And nature all o'ertasked to gain
A triumph for the mind.   I won
    That dear-bought victory, Sybelle,
Against most fearful odds.   The sun
    Day after day, and light that fell
From midnight moons, and evening stars,
And mornings gray through cloudy bars,
For months scarce noticed, came and went,
And found me still untiring, bent,
Soul, mind and body to that strife
    Of mind with might, to win the right.
That triumph won was won for life;
    But lost, had left me still in night,
    Groping and struggling for the light.
From that long, stormy war to rest,
A wearied child I sought the west,
And threw myself on nature's breast.
So many flowers were blooming here,
So many song birds charmed my ear,
I loved to lie beside the stream
And blend them all in one sweet dream,
Yourself among them.   Was it wrong?
Your song so like the thrush's song,
When it comes low and trilling through
The deep woods heavy with mist dew,

Foretelling soft, sweet summer rain;
  Your face so like your roses fair,
I own I felt a thrill of pain
  To find that you had thought or care,
More than your happy birds and flowers,
For life beyond your wildwood bowers.
Selfish! ungenerous!  In your eyes
I see the accusations rise.
Forgive, Sybelle, that selfishness.
When rest from thought to me was bliss,
I chafed to think of mammon's crown
Bending the dewy roses down,
Or thrushes singing for renown!
But all you ask is your own right,
Since even your roses seek the light,
And lovelier grow therein.  Now, strong
In mind and heart to right the wrong,
Such happy penance would I do,
As with my pupil wander through
The fields of thought that wide unroll
From history's almost magic scroll.
From the far dim and distant ages,
Grand prophet bards and hero sages
Shall meet us there; poetic fires
Shall flash again along their lyres —
That true inspired flame that leads
  Thought upward by its heavenly glow,
A fire from heaven, embalming deeds
  Of men whom gods were proud to know.
And kings of nature's royal race,
  Noblest among the sons of light,
Old kings of thought, who hold their place
  Secure by mind's divinest right

Above the sceptre, throne and crown,
Shall from their heights serene look down
Their blessings on our pilgrimage,
As wandering on from age to age,
We find the seed their hands have sown
To ripened fruit and vintage grown.
Those fruits we taste, that living wine
Shall make us like themselves divine —
Divine like theirs our lives to sow
With thoughts that shall immortal grow.
And harps of pleasant-sounding string
The bards of later birth shall bring —
Interpreters of life and thought,
Teaching us how the world is taught.
So shall you by their lessons learn
What fires on poet altars burn;
How they alone successful sing,
Who know with skill to touch the string
To which all human passions cling —
    The chord of human sympathy:
It vibrates to ambition's claim
The welcome, wished-for echo, fame;
It thrills to love's pervading flame,
    Though all unknown the hand may be
Whose fingers warm, from warmer heart,
The sympathetic fires impart;
It trembles deep to sorrow's moan,
Or lightly bounds to pleasure's tone;
And he the truest poet lives,
    Who, daring to be true and strong,
To human passions fearless gives
    Expression in ennobling song.

Fame on such brows her crown confers —
The world is proud of conquerors;
And life is better worth our breath
　　That they are born who dare to live,
Who scorn the coward's daily death,
　　And claim of life all it can give.


"Life and the world!   I feel again
Their call through strengthened frame and brain,
Warning the truant back.   Too long
He lingers in this vale of song.
Still, ere he go, he fain would dream
One summer hour beside the stream,
While yet along its tranquil vale
It woos the wild flowers bending pale,
Reading what strange, sweet prophecy
In its unresting depths may be,
And guiding with what skill he may
Its progress toward the brighter day
It seeks; till from the hill and glade
The slumbrous summer haze shall fade,
Till over wood and cottage wall
No more the harvest moonlights fall —
An hour of months, yet all too brief,
Till autumn drops her warning leaf,
Then, strong to measure might again
With iron wills of iron men,
His dreaming ends, himself content,
　　Nay, blest, if he one joy may give
To those sweet eyes upon him bent
　　In earnest asking but to live."

Slow from its forest dream awaking,
With noon's broad sunlight o'er it breaking,
Through all its waves, the streamlet clear
Trembles with joy akin to fear,
To find its ocean goal so near!

————

Sybelle, thou hast pressed to thy thirsting lip
A cup the bravest might fear to sip.
Was ever a goblet of brimming bliss
So crowned with the promise of life as this?
And did ever a mad bacchante clasp
A more fatal cup in her trembling grasp,
Or drain to the dregs from its rosy brim
Where she saw not the beaded poison swim,
With a wilder joy than thine eager soul
Hath grasped and will drink from this tempting bowl?
No voice to thy heart hath whispered of fear,
No warning floats up through the nectar clear,
Thou hast heard but the one endearing tone
That low to thy listening ear alone,
Hath said, it is life! Thou dost fearless stand,
With the wreathed and crownéd cup in thy hand,
Thy lips are pressed to the brim overflowing,
Deeper and warmer the rich draught is growing,
Richer and warmer its currents are glowing
Through all thy young being. What madness is
        thine,
To dream life alone can give joy so divine!

————

That hour of months was all too brief—
The thresher waits the ripened sheaf,

The summer's purple haze is gone,
The wan moon at the gates of dawn
Dethroned and sceptreless lays down,
Sad queen, her glorious harvest crown,
And fast o'er all the vale and plain
Fall autumn's warning leaves — in vain!

———

Low moans the sad autumnal gale,
    It will not let the dead leaves rest,
See one by one adown the vale
    It flings them on the streamlet's breast.

Poor withered leaves, poor silent stream,
    Together died your bloom and song,
How brief for you the summer dream,
    For you the autumn gloom how long.

The dreary winds moan sad and low,
    The dead leaves sink beneath the wave,
The streamlet murmurs in its flow
    As if it too would find a grave.

O murmuring one, thy ocean tomb
    Far in the future years will be,
And leaves will bud and flowrets bloom
    Along this silent vale for thee.

Low sounds November's latest sigh,
    Soft fall the snows above his bier,
And bloom and song and beauty die
    While winter shrouds the buried year

But life is wakening in the vale
  Again beneath the skies of May;
And June's sweet rose and lily pale
  Bend o'er the wandering streamlet's way.

Yet not one passion-dimpled smile
  Awakes for rose or lily fair,
And plaintive moans the brook the while
  Beneath the bloom and foliage rare.

But soft amid the summer light
  A mystic lay of love is sung,
O not for wild flowers wreathing bright
  Or leaves upon her bosom flung.

A cloud floats in the skies above —
  An angel presence, half at rest,
With soft enfolding wings of love,
  Deep mirrored in the streamlet's breast.

That sunbright cloud! how low it bends!
  What joy its heaven-born beauty brings!
With hers its being almost blends,
  It folds her with its shadowy wings.

From bank to bank the brook's sweet lay
  The thrilled and rippling ravelets bear;
She lingers on her tranced way,
  Her cloud love lingers in the air.

On her soft breast his image lies,
  And he for such sweet joy as this

Would almost leave his azure skies
   And melt amid those depths of bliss.

It may not be.   O bending cloud,
   Away — the parched earth calls thee now;
Amid the gathering storm-kings proud
   There is no prouder one than thou.

Away! thy lightning sword must flash
   In stormy scenes and stirring strife,
Where battling ranks with thunder crash
   Meet on the tented fields of life.

But ever 'mid that discord wild,
   Will come to thee in grief or wrong
The memory of the forest child,
   The wayward brooklet's love and song.

It may not be: alas, fond stream,
   Though mirrored in each trembling wave
Thoul't bear thy cloud love like a dream,
   A shadow to thy ocean grave.

With quiet songs adown the vale
   Thou still may'st chant thy hapless lay,
Beneath November's storm clouds pale,
   Beneath the blushing skies of May:

But dearer than the heavens above,
   Or summer flowers that round thee bloom,
The memory of that cloud-land love
   Thou bearest to thy ocean tomb.

# SYBELLE.

## PART II.

The sunset tints of amber light
Flame up the western skies to-night,
A broad, fair sea of burnished gold,
With cloudland shores around it rolled;
While like some glorious tropic isle
Where summer suns eternal smile,
One radiant star as day declines
Amid that sea of splendor shines,
An island heaven, where angels stand,
And wistful gaze on that far land
Whose cloud-enfolded mystery seems
The hidden goal of life-long dreams.
They see, slow moving to and fro,
The phantom shadows come and go;
They hear such music from afar
As never blessed their island star;
And bending o'er those crystal steps
Where calm the pallid twilight sleeps,
Wave far and wide their glittering plumes,
Till flashing o'er the distant glooms
They meet those beckoning forms of air,
And sink in silent darkness where

The rippling waves of melting gold
Around those cloudland shores are rolled.

O come thou cynic cold and stern;
Come vestal from thy burial urn;
Come cowléd priest, whose dream of life
At best is but a fearful strife,
A guilty barter on thy part
Of all thou hast of God or heart,
For living death in such a grave
As God to nature never gave;
Come watch the fires of fading day
Amid the gathering shadows play.
See how the daylight veils her face
With blushes in the night's embrace,
And how upon yon cloud's dark breast
The impassioned lightning finds its rest,
While bending from their thrones on high
The star-eyed angels smile to die,
If for such bliss their death atone
As visits not their Eden lone.
Though round their heaven such glory lies
They cloud-ward bend their longing eyes,
And trembling with a strange desire,
Slow raise their quivering wings of fire,
Forsake their thrones of light serene,
Speed o'er the amber deeps between,
And panting clasp those airy forms
To sink amid a night of storms,
More blest that wild desire to tame
Though darkness shroud their forms of flame;
More blest those quivering wings to fold

O'er pulses stilled and passions cold,
Than freed alike from bliss and pain
In yon empyrean pure to reign.


O what can virtue know of love,
When ice cold hands are clasped above
A bosom passionless as snow?
And what can love of virtue know,
When isolate, serene and lone,
It triumphs on its marble throne?
The deserts clasp their own green isles;
   To arid sands are fountains singing;
The blasted tree in verdure smiles
   With moss and vine leaves round it clinging.
The cold, bright icebergs borne afar
From realms beneath the polar star,
Give vigor to the languid breeze
That faints amid the tropic seas,
Then bend to meet the clasping wave,
At once their altar and their grave.
And lo, along yon clouded skies,
As mystic boreal torches rise,
Soft flashing o'er the deepening night,
They bathe the heavens in purple light,
Till earth, but now a darkened tomb,
Is blushing back a rosy bloom—
All thrilled and tremulous she glows
Beneath the light from arctic snows,
With flames more subtle, more divine
Than from the noonday splendors shine.


Who would forever gaze on heaven

If to its blue no clouds were given ?
Or bless the sun's eternal light
If nature gave no change of night? )
A stagnant pool the waveless sea
Within its silent shores would be;
And earth one broad Sahara made
Without its blended light and shade.
No flower of living joy may bloom
That springs not from another's tomb,
And life and love are only true,
When with the thorns and cross in view,
With patient strength and faith sublime
They dare the mount of woe to climb,
And brave death's dark ordeal through,
Its conquerors and its victims too.

What can they know of life who stand
Alone amid the desert's sand ;
Or shrink some cheerless cell within
To die of coward shame and sin ?
Even pleasure grasps her own sweet rose,
Though sharp the thorn beneath it grows;
The cross where martyred virtue prays
Alone is crowned with glory's rays;
And heaven's high portals are undone
Through suffering of the Sinless One.
The daring heart, the hand of steel
Alone the conqueror's joy can feel.
Then welcome nature's ceaseless strife,
Her life in death, and death in life,
And let the pale lips joyful press
The cup they have not strength to bless —

Life's bitter cup, where love divine
Hath mingled wormwood with the wine.

( O there be human hearts that crave
More of the world than just a grave ;
While life has so much more to give
They must have more than just to live.)
They would not breathe if breath were all
That bound them here in being's thrall ;
They cannot fold their hands and pine
Beside life's goblet brimmed with wine,
With thirsty lip  and longing eye
Dream that they dream, and dreaming die
To make life one long breathing lie.
Though all those purple depths may glow
With blended drops of bliss and woe,
With promise of but dregs at last
When the delirious draught is past,
It matters not : there be who drain
And  wish the  goblet filled again,
So sweet it is in life to prove
All hearts can know of life and love.

    Such mingled draught was thine, Sybelle,
Though drawn from love's enchanted well,
Though sweet with all its honeyed store,
With beaded kisses brimming o'er,
And warm with that most subtle power
Love has o'er life in passion's hour.
O sweet and warm on lip  and tongue,
And thrilling as the songs you sung,
Down to your heart the maddening draught

Went burning still and still you quaffed,
Till over lip and brow and brain
The fiery nectar flushed again.
And though the gall-drops blended there
Blanched from your cheeks the roses fair,
And clouded your calm, trustful eyes
With something of the world's disguise,
Though darker for the glory gone
The future's sunless years come on,
Still could your life go back once more,
As gladly, wildly as before,
With all that craving thirst of soul,
Your hands would grasp the proffered bowl,
And to the dregs, if dregs there be,
Your lips would drain it eagerly:
'Twere worth all life can know of pain,
To love and be so loved again!

No longer now within those eyes,
Or on that lip unanswered lies
The heart's great question.   O'er and o'er,
Each day more clearly than before,
Two hearts in conscious silence prove,
That love is life and life is love.)
What other power than love could throw
O'er all thy world so warm a glow,
Or wake within that sylvan dell
Such songs from thy sweet lips, Sybelle?

————

Open, O buds, to the light that is shining,
        Waiting and pleading to bless,
Pale in your pale hearts no longer repining
        Wake to the soft wind's caress.

Sunlight and south winds are pleading to you,
Night bathes your lips with her kisses of dew,
Morn gives you draughts of her balmiest rain,
Open, O buds of the valley and plain,
The summer is here in her fulness of bliss,
Why sleep through a life of such beauty as this?

Dreaming like you with life's light o'er me shining,
    Waiting and pleading to bless,
Cold in my cold heart I murmured, repining,
    Shrinking from beauty's caress —
Beauty that wooed me to nature's pure arms,
Crowded and crowned all my days with its charms.
Longing and dreaming of life more complete,
Scorning the perfect one cast at my feet,
And closing my eyes to its promise of bliss,
I slept as you sleep 'mid such beauty as this.

Welcoming now the pure light that is shining,
    Pleading no longer in vain,
Flowers that I scorned in my childish repining,
    Open to bless me again.
Winds that bring balm from the tropic isles blest,
Birds that sing low from the summer-full nest,
Grasses that quiver with life at my feet,
River full brimmed with the summer rains sweet,
Proud trees bending low in your stillness of bliss,
What spell hath enwrapped you with beauty like
    this?

Soft through the valley a splendor is shining,
    Softly and golden it falls,

Over the trees with their branches entwining,
    Over the low cottage walls,
Over the fields with their harvests and herds,
Over the blossoms, the river, the birds,
All nature so glowing and living in light,
Day giving warmth to the glory of night —
O heart how long darkened and dead to all bliss,
That lived and yet lived not in beauty like this!

As waking from a troubled dream
    Amid a world of light I stand,
By waters whose unfailing flow
    Gleams ever bright o'er golden sand.

I breathe a blessing on thy name,
    My guide to fountains so divine;
I drink, believing only life
    Can come from hand so pure as thine.

No mad bacchante's poisoned cup
    Is this that to my lip is pressed,
No rosy wine inspires such bliss
    As thou hast waked within my breast.

Thy words were like the prophet's wand,
    They touched the rock, and to thy side
How quick the living waters sprang,
    Delighted in thy sight to glide.

Now bending o'er the crystal wave
    I fill life's goblet unto thee,
And pledge thee by that love alone
    From thought of earthly passion free.

No bitter drops from Marah's stream
    Are mingled in the cup I drain,
And pure as thou to me hast given
    I give it back to thee again.

  O take it from the grateful hand
    That fills it brimming o'er for thee,
And pledge me by that love alone
    From thought of earthly passion free.

———

Blow soft and low, sweet southern wind,
Blow warm and low, and swift unbind
The fettered snowdrop; pale she lies,
Till thou unclose her sealéd eyes;
Pale in her cell the violet weeps,
And pale the sainted lily sleeps —
A poet dreaming over rhymes,
    With sweet bells waiting all in tune
To welcome in with fragrant chimes
    Thy bridal with the rose of June.
Sweet rose with thorns enguarded round,
And pale in clasping calyx bound,
No longer at thy emerald gates
The wind with patient wooing waits;
Though thorns may point around, above,
( Thorns pierce not half so deep as love.)
Stung by that passion-barbed desire,
With tropic breath and pulse of fire
Thy lover comes; along his way
The snowdrop fainted where she lay;
He kissed the violet's tears away;
He touched the waiting lily bells,

Their chime his waiting bliss foretells.
In vain in triple order stand
Those serried guards, a bristling band,
He comes to thee unharmed through harms,
He folds thee in his eager arms,
His sighs the calyx bands unpart,
His kisses wake and warm thy heart,
Till crimson blushes, self-confessing,
Thy willing lips to his are pressing,
And both, with clasp and sigh and kiss,
Rest perfect in your bloom and bliss.
How long the silent woods among,
The willow boughs in silence hung;
How pale, with life half understood,
The still flowers waited in the wood,
Or only stirred by passing wing,
Or by the fickle winds of Spring,
Till Summer came.   Sweet Summer wind,
Thy loves the forest tongues unbind:
Life breaks in bloom from shrub and tree,
The wild flowers flush and pale for thee,
And whisper low through all the grove,
O love is life, and life is love!
And low among her trembling leaves
Her own love song the willow weaves.

———

Come close within these clasping arms,
    O weary wandering Summer wind,
And let the lithe and drooping boughs
    Be with thy viewless being twined;
Then murmuring back thy whispered love
    And folded in thy dear caress,
This charméd life to both shall prove

One long sweet dream of blessedness.
Come closer yet; the willow bends
 Her glorious poet love to meet,
Her wreathing arms are round thee twined
 In fond caresses, wild as sweet.
Each quivering leaf that turns to thee
 Is witness of the love fires warm,
First fanned to life by thy soft breath
 And glowing sweet through all her form.
And each wild, passion-kindled song
 Thou hearest in thy minstrel tree,
Thy presence hath inspired alone —
 'Tis sung, O poet love, for thee!
Thy breath parts all the gloomy boughs
 Till golden noon from azure skies,
And morning's blush and evening's smile,
 And light from midnight's starry eyes,
And all the joy of beauty born,
 In earth or air, beneath, above,
So blended with thy presence seem
 That all alike awaken love.
Then while within the minstrel tree
 The willow's poet love may stay,
O wonder not she loves for him
 To weave the warm, impassioned lay;
That trembling in his clasping arms
 She yields her lips to his fond kiss,
In that long breathless draught that fills
 Her summer dream with perfect bliss!

———

Is it thy spirit, Love, that glows
 Through all the fervid summer air,

Filling the deep woods with repose
　　That is not rest — a yearning care,
A strange and tremulous desire
　　Thy own intensest power to learn —
A breathless longing for that fire
　　That all consumes, since it must burn?
There is no breath the leaves to move,
　　Yet quivering through the glowing hours,
In rapt unrest they bend above
　　The silent, upward-gazing flowers,
Flowers blushing at their own sweet glow,
And trembling though no winds may blow;
As she, the valley's fairest rose,
Alone where wild the river flows,
Blushes and trembles in her dream —
　　Her half-awakened dream of love,
Watching a vision of the stream
　　With its white bending cloud above.

On with ceaseless music ever
Sweeps and swells the restless river,
Deeper growing, swifter, stronger —
Ah, that guiding hand no longer
Turns at will the yielding current,
Checks or speeds the rushing torrent.

Toward the cloud up-gazing ever,
Smiles and sings the happy river;
He, an all too willing lover,
Beckons on and bends above her,
To her bright waves dimples bringing,
Paying kisses back for singing.

Whither, whither are ye tending,
Cloud and stream together blending!
Passion-blinded, maddened, dying,
But to quench that fiery sighing,
Burning cloud and throbbing river,
In the flame that burns forever!

On the gulf's dark brink the river
One brief instant pauses ever,
Breathless from its dream awaking,
Pauses ere that last plunge taking,
Down to depths where never, never,
Comes another dream forever!

Blinded by love's fatal kisses,
Will they see those dark abysses?
Lo, in music breathing ever,
To the cloud the waking river,
'Mid the white spray round her clinging,
On that fatal brink is singing.

Startled by the echoes wailing,
With her cheek now flushing, paling,
Fair Sybelle, from dreams awaking,
With that love-light round her breaking,
Where the warm rays glance and quiver
Sings beside the waking river.

"I who placed my hopes above
All that woman hopes from love,
In my eager grasp for fame
Plunged into the fatal flame.

What but love is this that turns
All my thoughts to one that burns
Lava-like through nerve and vein,
Filling soul and sense and brain?
What but love that makes the skies
Dark, when from those earnest eyes
Mine must turn with maiden dread,
Fearful lest the truth be read?
What but love makes every tone
Falling from those lips alone
Sweeter far than music's own,
Every smile that they have given
Dearer than my hopes of heaven,
Every word that they have spoken
Binding like a spell unbroken
Since I gave, in trusting hour,
Thought and being to their power?
Yielding to ambition's spell,
Drinking deep from learning's well,
I have drank of love as well.
Love! Whence came it? I nor sought,
Knew, nor dreamed it in my thought.
Childlike to his guiding hand
Mine I gave, and loved to stand,
Heedless of my flowers and birds,
Listening to his dearer words —
Dear, that to my wondering sight
They unveiled such worlds of light;
Teaching me that life is where
Soul and sense with being are,
Bounded not by realm or zone,
Crowded street or forest lone;

Drawing from the trees and flowers
Lessons sweet for summer hours —
Such as I had never known,
Though my life with theirs had grown;
Waking beauty from the sod
In the very path I trod;
Calling back the immortal dead
From the deathless page we read;
Grandest truth and noblest thought
From those lips new beauty caught;
Lowliest objects owned the spell
Where those words of music fell.
I, who loved the words, have grown
Strangely dear to prize the tone;
Strangely dear the soul to prize
Looking on me from those eyes
Bending oft so close above,
Offering life but taking love —
Taking, till mine eyes no more
See the future's shadowy shore,
For this ever blinding flame
Shrouding all my hopes of fame;
Taking, till my cheek grows pale,
And my throbbing pulses fail,
When his presence may not give
That sweet fire on which they live;
Till between the heavens and me
Evermore those eyes I see;
Till no other voice I hear,
Till that smile alone is dear,
And I tremble with a fear,
Strange and sweet as sorrow is

On the brink of happiness.
Still with sealéd lips and heart
I must act the pupil's part;
Listening, calmly as I may,
To his teachings day by day,
As he points with steady hand
Where ambition's votaries stand,
Girded strong the race to run
Ere their laurels may be won,
Urging me with purpose high
In their fame to share, while I
All would give if one caress
On that hand my lips might press.
Madness! folly! But this hour
Bend I thus to passion's power;
Back to life my soul must turn,
All these idle dreamings spurn:
Hiding in my heart alone
All of love that I have known,
Gathering round me, fold on fold,
Vestal garments pure and cold,
On ambition's nobler shrine
I must light the fires divine,
And beside that deathless flame
Sing alone for name and fame."

Ah, proud resolves, you lived your little hour,
Then drooped and faded as some fragile flower
Long nursed in shadows chill, may droop and fail,
When noon's full blaze falls on its petals pale!
(Ah, more than woman hadst thou been, Sybelle,
Successful to resist that wondrous spell

Love wrought upon thy woman's heart!) And more
Than man, or less, who daily bending o'er
The bright, up-glancing stream, could fail to know
His own form clasped in every wave, while low
His name blent ever with their murmuring flow.
Ah, more than man who had not longed to lave
Lip, brow and bosom in that swelling wave,
Who, thirsting unto death in deserts lone,
Would shrink to taste a fountain all his own!

Love's miracle of love, its life in life is this,
That breath of time that spans an age of bliss,
When eyes long gazing into eyes have learned
All that sweet wisdom by the stoics spurned;
When lips, long pressing sweeter lips, grow pale
Giving and taking, and the breath half fail,
The arms clasp closer, and the burning brain
Scarce dreams that virtue yet may warn in vain!
Blest they who on the gulf's dark brink have turned,
And, safe with all that dangerous wisdom learned,
Walked back to life more perfect, pure and strong,
Full of love's bliss, without its guilty wrong;
Warm with the breath drawn burning through each
        vein
From the sweet lips they dare to press again,
Full of the light from eyes more dear than heaven,
Strong with the strength that clasping arms have
        given,
By those dear arms and eyes and lips to prove
That perfect love is life, and life is love.

With all its perfectness of bliss endowed,

Proud in her happy love, and pure as proud,
Sybelle, the timid forest child, no more
Walks in vague dreams beside the river shore.
So many eves through all the summer's prime,
And glowing noons in golden harvest time,
So many morns of fading splendor drowned
In dreamy forest depths all autumn-browned,
So many months of days with loving hand
Has Raimond led her through historic land,
So long for her the poet's pages turned
While on his lips their inspiration burned,
So oft, so earnest to her eager mind
Life's purest aims, its noblest hopes defined,
Leading her thoughts still outward from her heart
To claim in great humanities their part,
That she has caught his spirit's higher tone,
And pure and strong in his strong nature grown;
Self-conscious of that strength too, but no less
A perfect woman in her tenderness.

And she has grown so beautiful: there lies
The light of that long summer in her eyes —
All that came down from the unclouded noons,
From the love-burning stars and tender moons,
Made softer, tenderer in those depths of blue,
By the loved eyes long gazing in them too.
The pure, fair cheeks, so rounded, clear and soft,
Change their bright rose and delicate tints so oft,
That love may read by his mysterious art
Quick telegraphic flashes from the heart.
(On the red lips they play too, those sweet fires,
To other lips like charged electric wires.)

All that warm bloom and half the blue eyes' light
Are woman's, love's own dower and beauty's right.
But round the tender mouth so firmly pressed,
In movements free, yet all so self-possessed,
In darker flames that sometimes light her eye,
In the firm calmness of her forehead high,
And in the voice, true prophet of the soul,
There lives and speaks, unconscious of control,
Strong in its gentleness, the spirit pure
That well can love and silently endure,
That half its strength and all its passion caught
From well learned lessons by her lover taught.
A beautiful, proud, loving woman — one
Whom Raimond has grown proud to look upon!
Part of his life, his very soul she seems,
As if his hand the ideal of his dreams
Had caught, and prisoned in that living form;
As if from his own lips, pure-breathing, warm,
Had gone the fires through all that lovely frame,
That gave such vigor to the kindling flame
Of thought, it might be genius, that so long
Found faint expression in her girlish song.
Kindling and glowing into life so new,
So strong, so beautiful her spirit grew,
So clinging to his own, and yet so free
From weakness in its fond idolatry,
That he had grown to love her with that love
Man knows but once, nor ever soars above
In all the flights his bold ambition dares,
Nor yet can crush with life-long crowding cares
Piled mountain high upon it: all between
Life's granite cliffs will cling its tendrils green,

3*

From fame's bleak pinnacle it blushes down,
The only rose twined in his laurel crown.

Thus, Raimond, though that love thou sacrifice,
Man-like, more free to grasp ambition's prize,
Thus will its deathless fragrance ever twine
Through all thy future life; and brightly thine
Will glow amid the laurel's troubled gloom,
In deeds born but of love's undying bloom.
Aye, go and join your battling ranks again,
Match your proud strength with strength of giant
       men,
Let other arms, long plighted, loved no more,
Welcome you nightly when the strife is o'er,
To gilded halls where desolate you roam —
*Her* gilded halls, your palace prison home.
Seek with *her* gold your woodland flower to hide,
Crush, trample on it in your march of pride,
( Still fresh it springs beneath your iron tread,
Acanthus-like — immortal from the dead! )

Is it her doom traced on his troubled brow
Sybelle is reading, gazing on him now,
With those dark flashes in her tender eyes
That change to purple black their azure dyes?
A strange o'ershadowing of prophetic wings
Seems darkening through the very song she sings,
Though firm and sweet and clear the music rings.

( "I sing for thee, love, a love song of the morning,
  It wakened my soul from its night dream of bliss,
Of thy lips on my eyes, love; O was it a warning
  That tears should be there in the place of thy kiss?

It springs from my heart as the wild bird is springing,
  'Mid dew drops and bloom from her own forest tree;
I'll sing it aloud as the wild bird is singing,
  In morning's sweet twilight I sing it for thee.

I sing it for thee ere the day god is sending
  His golden-tipped arrows of brightness afar,
While yet o'er his couch the night-mother is bending,
  Her pale forehead gemmed with one beautiful star.

Strange moment of doubt, when the worshipped ideal
  Seems purer and holier far than the true,
When we gaze on the rising but shadowy real
  Through mystical light born of starbeams and dew.

O love, might we grasp the loved forms that are flying,
  The visions that fade with the twilight away! —
Alas, in the light that reveals them they're dying,
  As night ever dies by the cradle of day.

Proud Night! as she bends o'er the god at his waking,
  His arrows are lodged in her beautiful breast;
She sinks mid the splendor that round her is breaking,
  And the stars have gone down to watch over her rest.

Farewell to thee, star-crowned and peerless Ideal,
  Farewell to the dreams that are buried with thee!
And welcome the strong-hearted, passionless Real
  That riseth in power as the night shadows flee.

It comes to the world like the sunshine, revealing
  What ages of starlight could never have shown; —

It comes to the heart by the lone grave of feeling,
   And sets its broad seal on the sepulchre stone.

It comes to me now as the day beam is shining,
   But sealed in my heart must its prophecies be,
For pale as yon stars in the twilight declining,
   Are fading the dreams I was dreaming of thee!

   " Blow free and strong, O winds of morn,
Blow far all dreams of darkness born!
Behold, on azure heights afar,
Fair shines the morning's herald star!
In silence deep on plain and steep
The shivering shadows closer creep;
The twilight dies in purple skies,
The white mist on her starry eyes;
And fair and frail above the vale
The night-long wandering moon grows pale.
Shine bright above, O star of love,
The purer coming day to prove!
Blow strong for right, O winds of might,
Blow wide the morning gates of light,
Blow far all dreams and doubtful gleams
Till perfect day above us beams! "

   "Too soon it comes, Sybelle; our dreams have
      grown
So sweet, so dear amid these twilights lone,
I could almost have wished no other bliss
In life, or other world or heaven than this.
Too soon — again those half-defiant flashes,
Sybelle, burn darkly through your shadowy lashes.

What mean they, love?   I saw them once before,
That sweet June night when by the river shore
You prayed for life, and thought your lips could
    press
Rich wine even from its dregs of bitterness.
They do; and from their own excess return
A richer wine where'er their kisses burn.
(Dear lips that give so much more than they take,
Close be they pressed to mine for love's sweet sake.)
I thought to teach you life, and I have caught
More from these lips than all the world has taught.
That sweet, sweet lesson let me learn again;
I thought I lived and you were dreaming then.
But both were cold, both dreamed, both waked, and
    now
I live in dreams and dream of life; and thou
Wilt never dream again, my own, ~~my~~ love;
God look in pity on us from above,
Come closer; pour in mine those dear, dear eyes,
Now warm with tender light of morning skies;
Forget that ever rising day may bring
For thee one black plume on his golden wing;
Forget, dear love, that pain or grief or wrong,
May jar one chord in all thy life of song;
(Forget that dreams like ours may end in pain;
Clasp me and say, I love thee, once again."

" Say that I love thee! must the joyous earth,
    In measured tones to the bright sun replying,
Tell of the love that in her heart has birth
    While she beneath his radiant smile is lying?
Is not each blossom eloquent with love?
    Each budding germ on her warm bosom glowing,

All mutely breathes to the blue heavens above
   Of love's sweet rapture through her being flowing.
Thou knowest thy smile is sunlight on my heart;
   Thou seest my cheek with love-warm blushes
      burning;
Thou knowest how tears into mine eyes will start
   For very joy, when thine are on them turning;
And dost thou ask me yet by words to prove
How dear thy presence is, how true my love?

Say that I love thee! Yes, the vernal sun,
   Earth's glorious lover in his azure heaven,
Ne'er blessed the world he deigns to smile upon
   With deeper joy than thou to me hast given.
Not by fond words of flattering tenderness,
   By vows that lips have made and hearts have
      broken;
But by thy spirit's perfect power to bless
   Through words of life and love thy lips have spoken.
(Love thee! O, love, life evermore to me
   Had been a cold, sad sense of being, lonely,
And lost and weary, without love and thee,
   Life without life, a drear existence only;
Now warm with bliss that cannot change to pain,
And light with light that grows not dark again.)

It is no sin to love, and tell thee so;
   Ours is no passion born of youthful gladness,
Flushing at once to summer's fervid glow,
   Dying as soon by its own burning madness.
Love found us with our senses all awake; —
   Thine from their world life, mine from their life
     seeming,

It wove round us no brittle chains to break,
    Or wax-like melt beneath the day's first beaming.
O love, our love can no more die in us
    Than God's light from the sun in mid-day heaven
(Though I might see no more, nor clasp thee thus,
    Though all now mine to other arms were given,
The life thou gavest me and the love I give,
Immortal both, in each must ever live.")

    To other arms! Sybelle, canst thou divine
Why shrinks thy lover from the clasp of thine?
Why, at thy words, through nerve and pulse and
      brain,
Shot the keen torture of some deadly pain?
Why the warm lips grow pale and cold as clay,
And cheek and brow as white and chill as they?
Why all the anguish of a life-long agony
Seems gathered into that one glance for thee,
As the white lips are on thy forehead pressed,
And thou one instant folded to his breast,
Then left, thyself half chilled, and pale and numb,
With the wild fears that o'er thy spirit come!
Aye; fold those cold hands o'er and o'er again,
Press them to your still heart and throbbing brain,
Rally your startled senses as you may,
Go out into the morning cold and gray;
The black, bare earth alone will meet you there,
The damp, sad pressure of the autumn air,
And heaven with all its stars and glory gone
And low with lead-cold storm clouds overdrawn.
Alone, alone! Your pale face grows more pale,
And down the leaf-strewn pathway to the vale

Your steps move strangely slow; the very air
Around seems heavy with the woe you bear.
A dread you feel and yet you cannot name,
Creeps slow, and dark and cold through all your
　　　frame
And gathers round your heart. Where now the
　　　light
And glow of love that made the morn so bright?
Dark bend the clouds, and dark along its bed
The stream, its sands with dead leaves overspread,
Flows mournfully; the leafless trees bend low
In silent listening to your words of woe.

　"A cloud through which, alas, no eye can see,
Is hiding all the heaven's sweet light from me.
I knew, I felt its outline faint and dim,
Slow darkening up the far horizon's rim,
Yet shut my eyes and would not see it grow,
And would not see the lightnings round me glow —
The fierce, bright flashes, and the gloom that came
More darkly after every blinding flame.
I might have known — alas, too well I knew
Such gloom and flame from happy love ne'er grew.
What secret power these elements have nursed,
Or when or how the fatal storm will burst
It matters not. I know that it must come;
I felt it in those arms, those cold lips, dumb
With sorrow that they dare not press on mine.
O love, if gall be mingled in this wine,
Both, both must taste its bitterest bitterness;
Both have so deeply quaffed: nor thou the less,
Nor I, long-thirsting lips have eager pressed,

To drain the bowl so brimming and so blest.
My life, my love, my Raimond, thou hast given
All my proud heart could ask for this side heaven !
My guide, my teacher; to my darkened eyes
Making earth bloom a glorious paradise.
I drank in knowledge from thy lips as flowers
In thirsty gardens drink the summer showers
And grow by them; and I grew up by thee
So proud, so fearless and so trustingly,
Molding  my very being into thine
Till my own nature seemed no more as mine,
But strong, and high, and noble as thine own ;
And thine so noble! O love, I had grown
Almost to worship ere I dared to love;
So high thy own life aims — so far above
All my weak fancy dreamed.  In very shame
I blushed that I had even thought of fame
Before thee.  Blank and aimless until then
All being seemed.  It cannot be again.
Teacher and pupil, each in each we grew
And each from each a new existence drew.
Love came to thee as knowledge unto me,
Transforming life.  How free, how gloriously
Thy soul came forth in that new being's dawn !
Thy form such beauty and such strength put on,
Such consciousness of joy in life as lives
Alone where love's pure inspiration gives
To heart and soul and sense and being all
They crave of bliss that fills but cannot pall
The senses. ( Thine, love, thine and mine all this —
Hearts, lips, and eyes, and arms, so filled with bliss
They never shall grow cold again. ) Mine own,

My life, thou canst not leave me thus, alone!
Alas, not mine to drown these rising fears,
The weakness and the blessedness of tears!
If honor bids thee go and me to stay,
I must look in those eyes and trusting say:
( Go, love, though light go out of heaven with thee,
Thou canst not take the light thou gavest me.
Or if ambition lure thy spirit far,
And love or I thine upward pathway bar,
I could, as brave as thou, that love lay down,
Nor dim by one weak tear thy victor crown.
That is not love that victim-like would bind
Love to its altar, fettered, shorn and blind.)
But O, not this, nor this; my soul would go
In widening circles farther from its woe!
A dark, dark thought I cannot speak for pain,
Lies like a terror on my heart and brain.
Love long confessed, and soul with soul as one,
Why still in word and thought the future shun?
Why call such life as this a dream, and pray
God's pity on us both, as if with day
Some horror came to blacken all our bliss?
Why on the very breath that gave love's kiss
Came warnings of dark plumes, and grief, and pain?
Why all my earnest words of love in vain?
In vain! alas, even as I sang there came
A shivering chill like terror through that frame.
I watched it all with love's most jealous eyes,
From whitening lips to whiter forehead rise;
I felt it in the cold, strong energy
Of fingers clasping mine unknowing why;
And that last glance of heart-wrung hopelessness —

O Raimond, were it mine thy life to bless,
And dying I could bless thee, I would die
Rather than see again that agony.
I think — and yet I will not — dare not — no!
Far from this brain thou maddening phantom, go,
With thy proud eyes, and heart and arms as cold
As are thy lands and piles of yellow gold!
What if thy proffered coins were piled so high
Ambition on them might mount to the sky?
Two strong, true, loving hearts before them rise
Yet higher, above, beyond those very skies.
Must-they be crushed, life stripped of all its charms,
That he, a skeleton in your cold arms,
May clink your gold, and call that wealth and fame
That brands his perjured soul with guilty shame?
Black, black the picture grows! I see it there;
Down the pale shoulders streams the long black hair,
Black all the garments, and the cheek's blank white
Gleams ghastly in the death-gift's yellow light —
That heritage that binds him to thy doom
And throws o'er me this shadow from the tomb;
Black, soulless eyes, yet cruel, cold and vain,
Their glance of triumph burns into my brain.
It shot through his that same, same baleful glow,
And it will part us yet! Alas, I know
Too well his haughty spirit's power to bend
His own strong will to gain the purposed end;
And well I know that firm, unshrinking soul,
Would soar through flame to gain its wished-for goal;
Nor love nor I his onward course could bar
More than the clouds the pathway of a star.
Is this man's love? O Raimond, is it thine!

Can gold or fame so far our love outshine,
That thou, betraying all my holy trust,
Canst bury all beneath that gilded dust;
Canst call its dreary gleam thy being's light,
And cheat thy heart of life's divinest right?
And I — I asked thee but for life, not this,
O love, thou more than life, and more than bliss!
To have the draught that I must drink or die
So dashed with drops of blackest agony —
Black! all is black! are not those mocking eyes
Opening upon me from these darkened skies,
Showing the trees that gave their summer charms
To autumn's gilding, blighting, blackening arms?
Proud trees! in vain your moanings through the air,
You paid the price for all the woe you bear!
Why stretch your arms in helpless wailing down
To the poor stream who holds your summer crown
Deep in her bosom, black and dead and cold!
Poor little stream! your sands of shining gold
Are blackened too, by once bright golden leaves
O'er whose dead forms your troubled bosom heaves
In mournful murmurings, yet ever presses
Closer and closer in its chill caresses,
As I the summer hopes that floated down
Into my being — love's most regal crown,
Glowing and purple with the life drops wrung
From the great heart that proudly o'er me hung,
Showering its wealth upon me, as the trees
Poured theirs on thee with every passing breeze!
O love, I rave! Such wealth of love and light
Could never die! Are not the sands all bright
And golden yet within thee, sighing stream,

As when the summer poured its ardent beam
Into thy breast!   The blessed rains will fall
And wash away this dark, death-seeming pall,
And thou wilt bear along thy glittering sands
Thy own sweet woodland song to other lands —
A song so wayward, deep, and strange and wild,
The world shall bend to hear the forest child,
And wonder whence such music came.   And thou,
Forgetting half the gloom that shrouds thee now,
Remembering all the splendor and the blaze
Of light and bloom that crowned thy forest days,
Wilt pour new joy upon the world; thy song
Will bless all hearts, and make the faltering strong!
(Love should make souls like pure, life-gladdening
        streams,
Not pools all blackened o'er with boding dreams,
Silent, and dark, and dead, and poisoning all
On whom their blighting exhalations fall.)
O lost to me, yet ever loved as lost,
I can but bless the star whose rays have crossed
My darkened path!   My Raimond, thou shalt know
The life thou gavest will outlive the woe
Of losing thee, though that go down to death,
And claim the last sigh of my parting breath!
God bless thee, love; and be His strength to thee
As the great love of thy true heart to me,
Ennobling all the future.   We must part;
O bitter words to come from woman's heart!
Yet bitterer far that life-long, dark remorse
Wrung from man's soul o'er honor's blackened corse.
No, Raimond! if that call thee from my side
And place within thine arms another bride,

Still go!   I trust thy love as I trust heaven ;
Not all in vain the lessons thou hast given."

———

Strong hands long locked in fetters sweet,
Unclasping nevermore to meet ;
Arms trembling with their last caress ;
Pale lips that nevermore may press
The lips their life went out on ; eyes
All blank and wild, as if the skies
Had lost the sun at noon, and night
Dropped black upon a world of light ;
Low, faltering words, the heart's faint knells —
This is the sum of love's farewells !

———

The world has gained a braver heart,
    A hand more bold and strong,
A soul more firm to battle for
    The right against the wrong,
Since from that woodland vale came forth
    The hero of my song ;
Came forth, endowed with woman's love,
    A love he could not claim,
For one who long in plighted faith
    Had waited for his name —
Whose hand the golden ladder held
    Whereon he climbed to fame ;
Came forth with such a blessing pressed
    On hand and lip and brow,
As consecrate them all for truth

By love's most holy vow —
A blessing hallowed through all time,
And ever fresh as now.
He cannot raise that hand for wrong,
Whate'er the guerdon be,
Nor falsely speak with lips that hers
Have sealed in purity;
He cannot hold within that brow
A thought unworthy thee —
Unworthy thee, beloved Sybelle;
Beloved not all in vain,
Since to the needy world he came
A better man again,
With more of faith in womankind —
Of man's success less vain;
A better man for having had
His own heart depths to prove,
To find though blinded passion soar
All reason's guards above,
It cannot touch with tainted breath
A pure and perfect love;
A better man for all the bliss,
Perhaps for all the woe,
That maddening passion half withheld,
Half given in tortures slow,
Had mingled in the goblet rare
Whose depths he might not know.
O wondrous love! not woman's cheek
A paler hue could wear,
Not woman's lip in agony
Could frame so wild a prayer,

As wrung his soul with anguish in
   That parting of despair!
O wondrous love, that steadfast still
   In her blue eyes could burn,
Bent over his, as sorrow bends
   Above a burial urn,
Then half-despairing, turns, alone,
   Life's fearful task to learn!
Alone, back to the needy world
   A purer man he came,
With holier motives to redeem
   The pledge he gave to fame —
Among the noblest of the land
   To write the noblest name.
Alone, she wanders in the vale,
   Alone beside the stream,
Half-wondering if the memories
   That all so real seem,
Are not her wild imaginings
   In some bewildering dream.
She holds one hand upon her heart
   To still its throbbing pain,
And one upon her brow to cool
   That almost frenzied brain,
And murmurs with those lips so pale —
   "'Twere sweet to dream again."
But he had said that nevermore
   To her a dream would come;
And must the brain that once could think,
   Grow by its waking numb?
And must the lips that once could sing,
   Forevermore be dumb?

No; she would sing the songs she wove
   From fancies long ago,
When by her own loved stream she lay,
   To watch its quiet flow,
And crushed the roses in her hands,
   And only dreamed of woe.

   "All the day long,
     With a ceaseless song
     And the whole night through,
     Down its path of blue,
A cascade falls over rocky walls,
In a far off wood where the giant trees
Wrestle with storms or the passing breeze,
Where never a banner has floated high,
Or a glittering spire looked up to the sky,
Where the sunlight softly flickers down
Through the summers green and the autumns brown,
And the cold bright light of the winter night,
And the tender sheen of the springtime green,
In changeful beauty glow and fall
Where the cascade sings o'er its rocky wall.

   "But skies and trees,
     And the changeful breeze
     Like the rocks are chill,
     As the cascade still
Pours the full tide of her passionate song,
Whether of happiness, grief, or wrong,
Into her own cold breast of stone;
And the murmurs low, and the saddening moan,

4

That echo back from that dark abyss
The cry of the spirit's loneliness,
Are measured over with weary pain,
And poured on her rocky heart again,
While a misty cloud, like a cold white shroud,
Is gathered close o'er her troubled breast,
To hide the passions that will not rest.

  ( " A cascade lone,
   With its wall of stone,
   Is the ceaseless strife
   Of my hidden life, )
And coldly the stream of my being falls
Over life's chilled and flinty walls,
And the moan of my spirit's loneliness
Comes ever up from the dark abyss;
I press it down with a cry of pain,
But it springs to my sealéd lips again,
And again is dashed to the heart below
Where the wild and passionate waters flow,
(And I draw a cloud, like a cold white shroud,
Between the world and my weary breast,
And long for a night of eternal rest." )

  " Wild November winds are sighing,
   Mournful, wailing winds of woe,
  Sad the darkened stream replying
   Murmurs through the valley low;
  Mourning over all the splendor
   Lost amid that autumn gloom,
  Mourning for the blossoms tender
   Dead on autumn's icy tomb.

Pale they saw the rose leaves falling
    Drenched with sorrow's chilling rain,
Faint they heard the willow calling
    For her summer love in vain.

"See they not the rose-heart glowing,
    Ruby-like amid the frost,
Life more strong within her growing
    Than in all the petals lost?
See they not the willow keeping
    Loving watch the stream above,
All her frame, for all her weeping,
    Golden with her summer love?
Winds of autumn cease your sighing,
    Cease your murmuring mournful river,
Truth and beauty are not dying,
    Love in them shall live forever."

O there be flowers all fair and frail
That shrink not from the autumn gale,
Full of the blissful summer past
They smile amid the wintry blast,
And smiling die, as if still dreaming
Of love's warm sunlight o'er them beaming;
No faded leaves are falling low,
No blight lies on their summer glow,
All fragrant breaks their parting breath
In love's sweet triumph over death.
And thus, with trust undimmed by tears,
Sybelle waits through the passing years,
Till long that well beloved name
Has graced the honored lists of fame.

Unscathed through 'trial's fieriest hour,
Untainted by temptation's power,
Worthy of all her worship past,
And all her love, she sees at last,
A nation's grateful homage done
To him, her purest, proudest one.
Once more she stands the stream beside,
At twilight hour, in maiden pride,
With all that tender bloom that speaks
Of tender memories on her cheeks,
And that dark purple flame that lies
So constant now within her eyes,
More darkly glowing, while her song
Floats calm and clear the vale along:

"Life is a welcome gift to those who stand
Strong-armed and free in youth's bright morning
　　　　land,
When the dark clouds of error's night are gone,
With fainter mists that dimmed the rising dawn,
And fair o'er all, the sun's unclouded ray,
Pours the warm light of truth's eternal day.

"A welcome gift to me, O life, art thou,
Crowning all nature and my being now
With thy most perfect fulness.　All I sought,
Or craved, or dreamed of in my wildest thought,
Thou givest — light and love and truth, and power
Through them to ask for fame — ambition's dower.

("It were enough to live but once to say,
I love! but once in all life's pilgrim way
That Mecca shrine to touch; but once to know
How bright in human hearts love's flame may glow.

Once and forever—here, O Love, thy bliss,
That what hath been but once, forever is!

"Forever thus with thee, my guiding star,
Whose rays fall on and bless me from afar,
Undimmed it glows; and purer that the years
Watching thy course to higher, nobler spheres,
Witness no faltering, no eclipses there,
To dim the promise of thy dawning fair.

"I were unworthy of thy love and trust,
Unworthy of myself, if in the dust
I could bow down with weak and wailing cries,
Making that life a sinful sacrifice
That heaven and thou have blessed with light and
    truth,
So craved and prayed for in my darkened youth.

"Love is the dawn of truth unto the soul —
Life's morn, and noon, and night—its perfect whole!
I knew thy dawn, thy glorious noon, O Love,
And through thy night by starry memories prove
That thou art life! To thy undying flame,
I wake in hope my song for name and fame!"

# ADELAIDE.

# ADELAIDE.

## PART I.

Beloved and bright, though to the world unknown
   As the small spring that from the hillside breaks,
Glad in the music of its childish tone,
   And in the life its purity awakes,
Now joyous in the April sunlight dancing,
Now on the stars, now on the blossoms glancing,
Such was the childhood of a gentle maid,
Such were the infant years of Adelaide.

Blest childhood! with thy smiles and artless mirth
   Thou crownest life's dark years with hope and joy;
Thou diamond pure in this dark mine of earth
   Where scarce a gem is free from sin's alloy!
Bright as the ray that shines from heaven upon thee
Ere earthly pleasure to her arms hath won thee,
Such be thy life, thou angel just from heaven,
Thou cherub to a mortal's guidance given!

Fair as the opening rose at dewy morn
   That bloomed in beauty by her cottage door,

4*

So fair was Adelaide; and she was born,
   When radiant June its greenest foliage wore;
When leaves on leaves among the vines were wreath-
      ing,
And summer flowers their richest fragrance breathing,
With perfume filled the rustic cot that stood
Like a lone hermit in the sheltering wood.

Alone it stood; yet in its loneliness
   A refuge was it for three loving hearts;
To them a shield from sorrow and distress,
   Far from capricious fortune's luring arts.
There lived they to the distant world as strangers,
There shared they each the other's toils and dan-
      gers, —
The high-souled Ellis, Mary his young bride,
And Ruth, his sister dear, in friendship tried.

His fortune lost by trust too oft betrayed,
   By bitter wrongs his high ambition checked,
Here found he in the tranquil forest shade
   A joy that prosperous fortune oft has wrecked —
The joy of life; the gladness too of knowing
What love for him in other hearts was glowing.
The joy of life! now would he scorn to claim
That glittering toy, the tinsel wreath of fame.

Each day the love that solitude endears
   He saw in Mary's rapture-beaming smile,
And Ruth, though yet almost a child in years,
   Seemed like an angel destined to beguile
From his proud heart each vain and wild emotion,
And soothe his spirit by her true devotion;

But now, a purer, holier joy than this,
Was Adelaide, the crown of all their bliss.

Thrice hallowed, loved and helpless infancy!
   Blessed in thy helplessness, thy strong defence;
Blessed in the tenderness that springs for thee,
   Blessed in thy beauty and thine innocence!
How wert thou welcomed, of all joys the dearest,
Thou light that still the humblest cottage cheerest;
For thee burned woman's love with purer flame,
And man forgot ambition, wealth and fame.

Yes; all ambition but the wish to bless;
   All fame but that which heaven itself ordained —
The heart's own praise; all wealth but happiness,
   And the dear treasures his own cot contained.
What festal light o'er scenes of splendor streaming,
What dazzling gems on brows of beauty beaming,
Could match the sunlight breaking o'er her rest
Who slept with that sweet babe upon her breast?

Through wreathing vines and forest branches green
   The rosy beams of summer morning smiled,
How brightly fell they on that cottage scene —
   The youthful mother and her first-born child!
How fair that cheek the snowy pillow pressing,
How soft those arms her infant's form caressing;
The father's heart throbbed with sweet hopes 'and
      fears,
And Ruth's dark eyes were filled with happy tears.

Affection true and holiest love were there,
   It sealed their lips as with a mystic charm;

O few and brief such raptured moments are
  When words would fill the bosom with alarm;
When silent bliss from heart to heart is stealing,
And cheeks and eyes such speechless love revealing,
Tears, tears will flow, for nature claims them then,
From woman's eyes and from the hearts of men.


And they were blessed, for not more lovely grew
  The fairest bud on summer's blooming brow,
By sunshine warmed and nursed with fragrant dew,
  Than Adelaide, their bud of promise now.
Life's opening rose in artless beauty smiling,
Their light of life, now all their griefs beguiling;
She was their joy when daily toils were done,
She was their starlight and their morning sun.


Soon fled those brief and blissful summer hours,
  And faster sped the autumn months away;
Stern winter passed, and spring's reviving showers
  Fell on the tender leaves and blossoms gay.
Again the summer sunshine trembled lightly,
Where through the leaves the streamlet glistened
      brightly;
Sweet June, the first of summer's dazzling train,
Came back to earth with all her charms again.


O radiant June, thou month of bloom and balm,
  Thrice welcome art thou to our northern clime!
What deep repose pervades the forest calm
  When spring's perfection joins with summer's
     prime!
Morn breaks upon a world of dewy splendor,
And night falls gently o'er the twilight tender,

Soft zephyrs fan the languid brow of noon,
And beauty sleeps amid the woods of June.

Thus in still beauty by the placid stream
    The oak, the willow and the aspen stood;
The rich wheat ripened in the golden beam,
    While, like a strongly banded brotherhood,
Line after line in emerald armor shining,
With lance and streamer to the earth inclining,
Stood the green corn; yet all invisibly
'Twas rising upward, upward toward the sky.

Oft sheltered from the noontide's ardent ray
    Would Ellis thankful o'er the landscape gaze;
Along the verdant slopes spread far away
    Stretched the soft outline of the summer haze.
There the bright river in the distance fading,
Here the tall oaks his lowly cottage shading,
And those rich fields, by his own toil subdued,
All cheered and strengthened him in solitude.

'Twas thus with Mary's fair hand clasped in his,
    He stood beneath the oak's embowering shade,
The smiles that spring from conscious happiness,
    And mutual love, upon their features played.
When music, clear as from the deep sky falling,
Came to their hearts, their own bright youth re-
        calling,
'Twas Ruth's sweet voice that through the green-
        wood rung
While thus to Adelaide she playful sung:

Child of the dark eyes
   And beautiful brow,
Bud of the wilderness,
   Why bloomest thou?

For joy in thy sorrow,
   For light in thy gloom,
For life and for beauty,
   Thus do I bloom.

Life is a moment,
   And joy ends in fear,
Bud of the wilderness,
   Why art thou here?

Emblem of Heaven
   Its truth and its love,
I show thee the beauty
   Of angels above.

Blest be thy beauty,
   And hallowed thy birth,
Bud of the wilderness,
   Welcome to earth!

# ADELAIDE.

## PART II.

How swiftly pass the bright meridian hours
    That measure manhood's years of ardent prime,
How few at noon will stoop to note the flowers
    That charmed them in the balmy morning time.
Still in the shade the blossom blooms as sweetly,
Matures and strengthens as the years pass fleetly,
And when the proud one droops in weariness,
Its love shall cheer him and its beauty bless.

Thus bloomed the gentle Adelaide; while years
    Brought added cares to Ellis' thoughtful brow,
And Mary watched with love's prophetic fears
    On Ruth's fair cheek the hectic beauty glow.
Nor watched alone; for other eyes were reading
That fatal page; another heart was pleading
That heaven in pity might avert the doom
And save its idol from an early tomb.

The young, proud Edmond, who for her sweet love
    Forsook the world, forgot his hopes of fame,

Nor knew nor cared to know a joy above
   Her humbler lot; and oh to hear his name
From such pure lips, to see her dark eyes beaming
With love so true, so angel-like in seeming,
Was more than life to him — 'twas his life's light,
Without whose presence all was death and night.

O it is beautiful, yet sad, to see
   How man's proud strength in gentleness can bend,
How it can cling with fond idolatry
   To woman's form, and with her being blend
Its life-long hopes; how, on her love relying,
He braves all dangers; but when she is dying,
He powerless falls, or, like the blighted oak,
Defies the storm and dares the lightning's stroke.

So Edmond fell, when from his clasping arms
   His promised bride, his gentle Ruth was torn;
So Ellis stood, when o'er her pallid charms
   He saw in grief his stricken Mary mourn.
From the sweet dream of love and hope awaking,
The lover raved, his weary heart was breaking;
While the calm brother, pale and tearless by,
Checked his own grief to soothe his Mary's sigh.

And Adelaide, the gentle, loving one,
   The watchful angel of the household band,
Forever present with her cheerful tone,
   Her words of love, her ministering hand,
How did she with strong purpose check the gushing
Of tears that ever to her eyes were rushing,
How did she strive with woman's tenderness
The maniac lover's hapless lot to bless.

Death changes not the dying only; no
   The living too are molded by his power,
As doth the fruit in full perfection grow
   Above the dust where sleeps the withered flower.
So in the maiden's heart new strength was springing,
New thoughts were there, a holier purpose bringing,
At once from her the bloom of life was gone,
At once the destiny of woman won.


She felt what hearts like hers but once can feel —
   That she had loved! With what a mad'ning pain
Did that dread truth upon her spirit steal!
   How did she strive to banish it in vain!
With every thought of girlhood's hours of gladness
Was linked his name; and though it now were mad-
      ness,
Though hope was dead, and reason's sun was set,
True to her destiny she loved him yet.


But oh, with such a chastened, fearful love
   As seldom girlhood's guileless heart has known;
She would not wrong the sainted one above,
   To wish one thought, one smile, one tone,
Of all the blissful past to her were given,
Or could be hers; not for her hopes of heaven
Would she to mortal eyes the love unveil,
That preyed upon her heart, that made her young
      cheek pale.


It was enough that through the weary years
   His blighted spirit might be doomed to live,
Her voice could cheer, her presence calm his fears,
   Or to his life one gleam of pleasure give.

It was enough amid that night of sorrow,
One ray of light, one trembling hope to borrow
From his sad smile, when wandering by her side,
He talked of Ruth, and called her his lost bride.

He told her that when years of grief were spent,
    And he had wandered many a weary way,
When his lithe form with feeble age was bent,
    And his dark locks were sprinkled o'er with gray,
Then should he find her, just as she had vanished,
When light and beauty from his life were banished;
And she who loved him with such holy truth
Could bring him back to beauty, strength and youth.

He was a gentle maniac, and his eye
    Had more of sadness than of reason lost;
As if the star that lights the morning sky
    By dark'ning clouds and sudden storms were cross-
        ed.
Still shines the star, and though so dimly beaming,
One watchful eye still marks its fitful gleaming,
One heart yet hopes, when storms have passed away,
Its light shall dawn upon a happier day.

That happier day! When shall its dawning be!
    Alas, the clouds are threatening deeper gloom;
And Adelaide, thy star of destiny
    In dark eclipse seems hovering o'er the tomb.
By the low couch, in prayerful sorrow bending,
Despair and hope are in thy bosom blending;
Hope for the spirit feebly struggling there,
Hope for the mind, but for the life despair!

O patient watcher, thy fair brow is pale,
　Thy native rose blooms on thy cheek no more.
A year has passed, and now the autumn gale
　Sweeps with sad wail the cheerless landscape o'er
All nature dies, and lo, before thee lying,
The one thou lovest all too well seems dying.
No cloud of mental gloom, no madness now,
Dims his clear eye or darkens his pale brow.

And he is looking up to thee; his hand
　Clasps thine; he faintly murmurs, "Adelaide."
Dear is that voice to thee as breezes bland
　Unto thy emblem rose of June, sweet maid!
Bend low; the rose bends when the breeze is singing;
Bend low; the rose bloom to thy cheek is springing.
O child of hope! thy fervent prayer is heard;
'Tis answered by that softly murmured word:

Another June with its blue, cloudless skies,
　Its shadowy forests and its world of bloom,
Its sparkling stream that now in sunshine lies,
　And now is lost amid the greenwood gloom —
Another June, and Edmond's cheek is glowing
With health's warm hue; through azure  channels
　　flowing,
The rich blood tints the lately pallid brow,
So dark with sorrow once — the throne of reason now.

And there is music by the stream once more —
　A sound of song upon the breezes flung;
Not the soft notes of Ruth's sweet voice of yore
　When to the infant Adelaide she sung.

But manlier tones with deeper cadence thrilling,
And the fair listener's eyes with radiance filling.
Tis Edmond sings, and Adelaide is near,
Nor lists she now with thoughtless childhood's ear.

The ocean wanderer loves the star
        That guides him to his home ;
Though oft he views the meteor lights
Or on the billow's crested heights
        Admires the sparkling foam,
    He heeds them not, but turns away,
        And heavenward looks so wearily,
    To where the only light he loves
        Beams o'er his path so cheerily.

The traveler 'mid the desert sands
        The green oasis sees,
And what though gems from every mine
In tempting radiance round him shine,
        More dear to him the breeze
    That marks the fluttering palm tree nigh,
        Beneath whose shade untiringly
    The fountain springs, and warbling birds
        Sing to his heart inspiringly.

A wanderer I on life's dark sea,
        A traveler 'mid its sands;
The star I loved has set in gloom,
And where I saw the oasis bloom
        A mocking mirage stands.
    I cannot love that darkened sky,
        The desert winds blow chillingly,

And life bereft of love might turn
And welcome death most willingly.

Yet from that dreary ruined past,
My Adelaide, to thee,
To thee, beloved from early years,
To thee, whose smile my spirit cheers,
I turn for sympathy.
No wealth or power I offer thee,
To tempt thy heart beguilingly;
I only ask that for my love
, Thou'lt look upon me smilingly.

I cannot say that sad regrets
Will never cloud my brow,
But while thy voice can charm my ear,
And while thy loving eyes are near
To smile on me as now,
How can I choose but bless the day,
When wildly and despairingly,
I looked on death, and, but for thee,
Had left the world uncaringly?

For thou hast won me back to life,
To life, to love and thee;
My Adelaide, beloved and blest,
To thee the wanderer turns for rest,
For love and constancy.
No fame or rank I offer thee
To tempt thy heart beguilingly,
I only ask that for my love
Thou'lt look upon me smilingly.

Her eyes are raised, their light has met his own;
  To him their tearful lustre far outspeaks
The loved and gentle music of her tone,
  Or the deep tints that stain her glowing cheeks.
It is enough, the blush and tear are telling
All the fond hopes within her bosom swelling;
Enough — her long-tried love is well repaid,
The tale is told; farewell sweet ADELAIDE.

# MARGUERITE.

You wonder why I sing no more,
　　But coldly at your feet
Stand gazing up into your eyes,
With something like a strange surprise,
And make no flattering, sweet replies,
　　When you are speaking, Marguerite.

You love my simple rhymes, you say,
　　And urge me to repeat
The boyish tale I used to tell,
When wandering in the hazel dell,
Where soft the summer twilight fell,
　　When we were children, Marguerite.

Alas, we are not children now,
　　And trust me, 'tis not meet
That I, an humble country swain,
By rustic rhymes should hope to gain
What nobler bards have sought in vain —
　　One grateful smile from Marguerite.

I've watched you when their tender strains,
　　With flattery's incense sweet,

Might well have brought each latent grace
That in a maiden's soul hath place,
To smiles and blushes on her face,
  You did not hear them, Marguerite.

Your brow was like the marble cold,
  And when they turned to meet
The guerdon of your gentle smile,
You seemed as lost as if the while
In some far off enchanted isle
  You had been dreaming, Marguerite.

When such have failed, what hope have I,
  The lowliest at your feet,
To win one glance from your dark eye,
To wake within your breast one sigh,
Or on your lips one kind reply
  To my poor song, proud Marguerite?

You are no more the joyous child
  Who in life's spring-time sweet,
Could roam delighted by my side,
With no high dreams of wealth and pride,
Or such proud scorn as can divide
  The loved and loving, Marguerite.

But calm beyond the charmèd line
  Where child and woman meet,
With pride enough on lip and brow
To make a king in homage bow,
In all your glorious beauty now,
  I see you standing, Marguerite

I would not from your worshiped eyes
    The cold indifference meet,
That chills the fire on passion's tongue,
Checks lovers' songs ere they be sung,
And sends your devotees heart-wrung
    From your proud presence, Marguerite.

I hide within my heart of hearts
    That dream so pure and sweet,
The boyish love of life's young morn
Shall never meet your cruel scorn,
It dies as silent as 'twas born, —
    Why are you weeping, Marguerite?

Can tears wash out the cold disdain
    With which you loved to greet
The pleading eyes to yours upturned?
And has your haughty spirit learned
How deep their fires of passion burned
    By your own tortures, Marguerite?

O blessed tears! my boyhood's dream!
    In maiden beauty sweet,
Down from your cold and distant throne,
With love long kept for me alone,
Into my arms, my own, my own!
    Those tears have brought you, Marguerite!

5

# LILLIAN GRAY.

By yon low grave where Lillian sleeps,
And where the drooping willow weeps,
   The wild birds love to stay;
They meet around her in the night,
They sing of her at morning light,
   I hear them all the day;
But O it seems a weary song
To hear them singing all day long,
   We mourn for Lillian Gray.

Within that grave my Lillian sleeps,
Above her head the willow weeps,
   She has no sculptured stone;
But day by day an artist old,
Is graving with his fingers cold,
   My heart, to marble grown;
And all the name he traces there
From dewy morn to evening fair,
   Is, Lillian Gray, alone.

# LILLIAN GRAY.

Beneath the tree that o'er her weeps
I'll lay me where my Lillian sleeps,
   To guard her while I may;
For sterner seemed that form of fear
That traced the name of Lillian dear
   Upon my heart to-day.
I'm dying, and the wild birds sing
Above the monument I bring,
   To thee, my Lillian Gray.

# AMY DEAN.

With lingering steps day after day
I've passed your cottage garden gay;
I've watched the blossoms of your care
So sweetly nursed and tended there,
Your roses in their summer glow,
Your lily bells like perfumed snow,
Your poppies flaunting in their pride
The daisy's modest bloom beside,
The violets in their green retreat,
Sweetwilliams gay, and pinks more sweet,
Yet ne'er a lovelier blossom seen
Then your own self, sweet Amy Dean.

Beside your cheek the roses fade,
The saintly lilies droop in shade,
When near them your white brow is bent
So pure in its serene content;
The pinks where late the wild bee sips
Have no carnation like your lips,
They bend before such rivals sweet,
And pour their fragrance round your feet.

The violets with their eyes of blue
Look up most sister-like to you,
Yet bolder in their coverts green
Than your own self, sweet Amy Dean.

Prim in their Puritanic ways
The worshiping sweetwilliams gaze,
With all your bloom, but not your grace,
Up to the heaven of your face.
The poppies bow their heads of pride
To touch your garments as you glide
So lightly down the garden aisles
To meet the daisies' morning smiles.
All flushed with pleasure, like that flower,
I've watched your coming many a hour,
And, trembling, wished my lips had been
The leaves you kissed, sweet Amy Dean.

You gave me once, with timid grace,
And blushes mantling o'er your face,
A rose bud pale; I begged the gem
For it had touched your garment's hem;
I thought it then a Crœsus' store ;
Now, miser-like, I ask for more.
Not for your daisies gemmed with dew,
Your lily bells, or violets blue,
Sweetwilliams prim, or poppies gay,
Or perfumed pinks that crowd your way ;
I ask but one, the garden's queen,—
Rose of my life, sweet Amy Dean !

# MY MARY.

How softly steal the twilight shades
　　Along the pale September sky;
How purely bright the diamond dews
　　Among the clover blossoms lie.
At this sweet hour when toils are o'er,
　　And homeward hies the weary bee,
I know beside my cottage door,
　　My bride, my Mary waits for me.

The clover bloom is on her cheek,
　　And in her eye the diamond dew,
And ne'er in virgin bosom beat
　　A heart more loving pure and true.
She thinks her hunter strangely late
　　As shadows lengthen o'er the lea;
And now beside my cottage gate,
　　My gentle Mary waits for me.

The bloom is fading from her cheek;
　　Her eyes are dim with starting tears;
When lo, adown the forest path,
　　My Rover's welcome voice she hears.

She strives to pierce the gloom in vain,
   For darkness deepens round each tree ;
And now along the shadowy lane,
   My trembling Mary flies to me.

My Mary! 'tis not fear that gives
   Such fleetness to her steps to-night,
That makes her press so close to mine
   Those balmy lips and eyes of light!
My cottage by the wood no more
   My happy cottage home would be,
If at the lane, the gate, the door,
   My Mary might not wait for me!

# JENNY.

Of all the farmers' girls I know,
   And they, to say the truth, are many;
There's scarce among them one, I trow,
   In all things can compare with Jenny.

Jenny with the laughing eyes,
   And her darkly braided tresses;
Jenny with her fairy form,
   And her dainty foot that presses
Lightly as the leaves that fall
   On the grass from boughs above her;
Would that you my Jenny saw,
   For you could not choose but love her.

She can spin and knit and sew,
   With those fingers fair and slender;
She can mould the whitest loaves,
   And bake them brown and tender.
And the cows at morn and eve
   For her coming look with pleasure,
Yielding to her skillful hand
   Richest milk in flowing measure.

At her call the lambkins run
  Down the clover paths to meet her;
For her care the garden blossoms
  Send their sweet perfumes to greet her.

Never over her dear face
  Discontent its gloom is flinging;
And she sings as honey bees
  At their own sweet work are singing.
In that little head she bears
  Such a wondrous stock of knowledge,
That were I to tell you half,
  You would think she'd been to college!
But if I should sing a month,
  Praising her above the many,
You would never be content
  Until you had seen my Jenny.

There may be scores of city girls
  Can boast of fairer faces,
And forms more shaped to fashion's mold,
  Tricked out in silks and laces.
And useless fingers lily fair
  With gilded trifles playing,
And rosy lips, and languid eyes,
  May tempt young hearts a-straying;
But if from these you turn aside,
  A wiser man than many,
And seek a WOMAN for your bride,
  Perhaps you'll find my Jenny.

# JOSEPHINE.

How like a blossom fair and frail,
　Is she I love, my bosom's queen;
My fragile lily of the vale,
　My gentle Josephine.
So fair, so pure, so frail she seems
　I dare not half my passion own,
Lest, like the angel of my dreams,
　I wake to find her flown.

I've seen the tender flower of spring
　With such unconscious blushes dyed,
When low the amorous breeze would sing
　What I to speak have tried.
I've watched it still as flushed and pale
　It trembled to the breeze's sigh,
Then drooped, while listening to the tale,
　In virgin bloom to die!

And thus I fear my ruder love
　Would crush the blossom I would bless,
I dare not ask the one sweet word
　To seal my happiness;

So like a blossom fair and frail,
  Is she I love, my bosom's queen,
My fragile lily of the vale,
  My gentle Josephine.

# LITTLE ALICE:

Blow soft, ye gentle summer winds,
   Round the dear home where Alice dwells;
Waft to her songs of happy birds,
   And odors from sweet lily bells.
Fan the pale roses on her cheeks
   To rosier bloom each coming day,
Kiss her young lips and forehead fair,
   And through her clustering ringlets play.

She is the one sweet bud of hope
   To bloom upon the household tree,
Deal gently with her, winds of heaven,
   Unfold the blossom tenderly.
May no rude storm or fatal blight
   Reach the dear home where Alice dwells,
Amid the songs of happy birds,
   And fragrance from the lily bells.

# ESTELLE.

How motionless, how pale she stands,
A statue cold with icy hands
Clasped tightly o'er a breast of snow;
And but that oft her dark eyes glow
With the strange fire that fills them now,
And wreathes with living light her brow,
She might be what at times she seems —
A thing to haunt your midnight dreams,
An iceberg worn by wind and storm
Till moulded to a woman's form,
Then left, a monument of rest,
On some lone isle in ocean's breast.

But words are on her parting lips;
Her soul seems waking from eclipse:
For name and fame! The words are said,
And the deep thoughts unto them wed,
Are burning in her eye's dark flame,
And on her brow — for name and fame!

Back to her cheek with quivering start
The life blood rushes from her heart —

So cold, so beautiful, it glows
Like sunlight on the polar snows.
That blush becomes thee passing well,
O gifted, proud, and cold Estelle!
Yet those who know what passion wrings
The heart from whence such beauty springs,
May well the glorious boon forego,
And lose its charm to shun its woe.
Thy pallid lips so closely pressed,
Thy still hands folded o'er thy breast,
Thine eye unblessed by feeling's tear,
Thy brow so cold, so calm and clear,
Show that no thoughts of pleasure came
With those wild words, for name and fame!

What hope is thine of earthly joy
That time can blight or death destroy?
For thou hast bowed in dust to mourn
The idol from thy bosom torn;
The cheerless grave has closed above
Each object of thine earthly love.
Behind, each path that promised bloom
Hath led thee by an open tomb;
Life's troubled ocean spreads before,
And thou upon its lonely shore
Hast listened to its moans so long
Thy lips would echo back its song!

Now Fame her brightest wreath may twine
Around that marble brow of thine,
And worshipers on bended knee
Their flattering homage pay to thee;

But laurel crowns could never press
A brow more cold and passionless,
Nor shrinéd idol calmer stand
Amid her kneeling, votive band.
No word of praise, nor passion glance,
Can wake thee from that statue-trance ;
And but the waves that round thee moan
In echo to thy answering tone,
Can quench in death thine eyes' dark flame,
And still thy song for name and fame.

# ROSE OF EVANDALE.

O Rose, fair Rose, my blooming Rose,
    My own sweet Rose of Evandale!
What care I for the lotus bloom,
Or for the violet's sweet perfume,
    What care I for the lily pale,
While I can feast my ravished sight
On thy dear cheek with blushes bright,
    My peerless Rose, my blooming Rose,
    My own sweet Rose of Evandale!

The walls that guard my chosen flower
    Are mountains capped with snow-clouds pale,
And many a winding streamlet glides
In beauty down their verdant sides,
    To meet and mingle in the vale,
Where dwells one ever-blooming spring,
And birds in charmèd numbers sing
    To thee, fair Rose, my blooming Rose;
    My own sweet Rose of Evandale.

A bower is by the stream that winds,
    In ceaseless music through the vale,

And thronging there, of every hue,
In wreathing garlands pearled with dew,
    A thousand blossoms scent the gale;
But brightest of them all is she,
The peerless Rose that blooms for me,
    My heart's sweet Rose, my blooming Rose,
    My own dear Rose of Evandale.

# KITTY'S CHOICE.

A wealthy old farmer was Absalom Lee,
    He had but one daughter, the mischievous Kitty
So fair and so good and so gentle was she,
    That lovers came wooing from country and city.
The first and the boldest to ask for her hand
    Was a trimly dressed dandy who worshiped her—
        "tin;"
She replied with a smile he could well understand,
    *" That she'd marry no Ape for the sake of his*
        *skin !"*

The next was a merchant from business retired,
    Rich, gouty and gruff, a presuming old sinner; —
Young Kitty's fair form and sweet face he admired,
    And thought to himself, " I can easily win her."
So he showed her his palace, and made a bluff bow,
    And said she might live there, but wickedly then,
Kitty told him she long ago made a rash vow,
    *" Not to marry a bear for the sake of his den !"*

A miser came next; he was fearless and bold
    In claiming his right to Miss Kitty's affection;
He said she'd not want for a home while his gold
    Could pay for a cabin to give her protection !

Half vexed at his boldness, but calm in a trice,
    She curtseyed, and thanked him, and blushingly
        then,
Demurely repeated her sage aunt's advice,
    " *Not to marry a hog for the sake of his pen!* "

The next was a farmer; young, bashful and shy,
    He feared the bold wooers who came from the city;
But the flush on his cheek, and the light in his eye,
    Soon kindled a flame in the bosom of Kitty.
" My life will be one of hard labor," he said;
    " But, darling, come share it with me if you can."
" I suppose," she replied, gaily tossing her head,
    " *I must marry the farm for the sake of the man!* "

# ROLAND AND ROSALIE.

A wild red rose was blossoming
  Upon its bending spray,
Beside a sparkling woodland spring,
  Beneath the skies of May.
Around its stem their golden bells
  The early cowslips hung,
And drowsy bees in every cell
  Their dreamy murmurs sung.

A rippling brooklet from the spring
  Went wand'ring on its way,
Among the cowslips' golden bells,
  Beside the rose of May.
And two fair children, like the stream,
  In life's unfettered hours,
Came out beneath the spring's soft beam
  To play among the flowers.

The blooming cheeks of Rosalie,
  And Roland's golden hair,
Were lovelier than the rose of May,
  Than cowslip bells more fair.

The sunlight glancing on the wave
   Ne'er woke a brighter smile,
Than beamed from his soft azure eye,
   And wreathed her lips the while

They scared the wild bees from their cells
   Beneath the bending spray,
And with the cowslip's golden bells
   They twined the rose of May.
And Roland bade fair Rosalie
   Her gentle head bend low,
The while he bound the braided wreath
   Above her brow of snow.

"Now list thee, Roland," said the maid,
   " This broad green leaf shall be
A fairy boat to bear thy hopes
   O'er life's uncertain sea.
And this small petal, golden-hued,
   An argosy of mine,
Shall fear no wreck by wave or storm,
   While floating close to thine."

"So may they float, dear Rosalie,"
   The noble Roland said;
And side by side adown the stream
   The fairy vessels sped.
And down the broader stream of life,
   Two barks, launched side by side,
Went long ago proud Roland Vere
   And Rosalie, his bride.

# MY ROSE.

The flower I love best is no delicate blossom;
  Tenderly nurtured in luxury's bower,
Fit only to bloom on a lace-covered bosom,
  And flaunt in the glare of the ball room an hour.
No; out on the prairie my wild rose is growing,
  Fanned by the free winds that come from the
      west,
The warm hue of health on her bright cheek is
      glowing;
  My wild rose of beauty, the Rose I love best.

The maiden I wooed was no exquisite fairy,
  Fragile and dainty, and useless as fair,
To bask in the light like a gossamer airy,
  And vanish away at the shadow of care.
No; brave in her loveliness, like my wild blossom,
  She smiles through the storms that have broken
      my rest,
Bringing comfort and balm to my desolate bosom,
  O such is the Rose I have clasped to my breast

# A SONG FOR THEE.

A song for thee, thou joyous child,
  So lightly bounding o'er the lea,
With heart so pure, and laugh so wild,
  A merry song for thee!
All day the blue bird gaily sings,
  The robin makes his vespers long,
And warbles still with folded wings
  For thee a merry song.

A song for thee, thou maiden fair;
  Of hope and joy thy blue eyes speak,
Spring's earliest buds are in thy hair,
  Its bloom upon thy cheek.
Thou standest by a charméd stream,
  And low its murmurs sing to thee,
Of youth's sweet prime, its morning dream,
  And angel purity.

And thou who at the maiden's side
  Art pleading now with words so sweet,

Now half subduing manhood's pride,
 And kneeling at her feet;
Thou would'st not list with half the joy
 To harps, though strung and tuned above,
As when with lips so bright, so coy,
 The maiden sings of love.

A song for thee, thou matron dear;
 There's beauty on thy placid brow,
Thy dark eyes moist with many a tear
 Are yet all lovely now.
Thy children come with songs of mirth,
 To thee their cheerfulness impart;
No joy can be in all the earth
 More welcome to thy heart.

A song for thee, thou mourning one, —
 Ah, no; while bending o'er the grave,
Thou hearest but the sullen moan
 Of sorrow's whelming wave.
Earth has no music now for thee,
 No power to charm thy heart's despair;
God must thy only refuge be,
 Thy only solace, prayer.

A song for thee, thou man of years,
 Thou too art bending o'er the tomb;
Methinks thy waiting spirit hears
 The angels call thee home.
A blessing on thine aged head,
 Thy spirit still is pure and young,
And soon its pinions will be spread
 Those angel bands among.

A song for Heaven the home of love,
  The home of innocence and truth,
A song for those who meet above
  In their immortal youth!
Our life the strange, wild prelude seems
  To Heaven's undying minstrelsy,
And death the note that breaks our dreams,
  And sets the spirit free.

6

# TO SUMMER.

Stay thee, gentle Summer, stay; -
Haste not thus so soon away.
See, the skies are blue above,
Wooing thee with smiles of love.
Blossoms beautiful and bright
Throng around thy path of light,
While the bending forest trees
Stoop to hear the whispering breeze,
As its murmurs seem to say,
Gentle Summer, stay, O stay !

Morning in her radiant car
Woos thee from the hills afar ;
With alternate hopes and fears,
Smiling now and now in tears,
See she flings her balmy dew,
Fresh from yonder vault of blue,
O'er the parched and drooping grass
Where thy glowing footsteps pass,
And with sighs she seems to say,
Gentle Summer, stay, O stay !

Noon hath brought thee robes of light,
Wove with clouds and sunbeams bright,
And thy pure and dazzling brow
Beams in cloudless beauty now.
See, he looks on thee with pride —
Summer, thou'rt his chosen bride;
Do not from his presence fly,
See, the love that lights his eye,
Half commanding, seems to say,
Stay thee, gentle Summer, stay!

Evening flings her splendors free
O'er the sunset skies for thee
See beside the sparkling rills
Where the clouds have kissed the hills,
Stands she now with matron grace,
Wooing thee to her embrace.
Rest thee, beauteous Summer, rest,
In the crimson curtained west,
Haste not thus so soon away,
Stay thee, gentle Summer, stay.

Night hath spread her ocean blue,
Gemmed with isles of golden hue;
Billows sleep in silence there;
Cloudless all that sea of air;
Save one shadowy sail afar,
Moored beside its island star.
Lovely Summer, if thou go,
Storms will rise and tempests blow;
Wrecked will be that fairy sail
If it meet the autumn gale;

6

Haste not then so soon away,
Stay thee, gentle Summer, stay.

Vainly morning spreads her feast
In the bright and balmy east;
Vainly o'er the hills afar,
Evening lights her beacon star;
Vainly with his luring wiles
Noon in manhood's beauty smiles.
O'er her placid azure deeps
Night, the jewelled goddess weeps —
Vain the smile, and vain the tear,
Summer may not linger here.

Clouds are darkening round thy way;
Summer, here thou canst not stay.
Higher, darker still they rise,
Mountains floating in the skies.
Speed thee on thy pathway now,
Summer with the dazzling brow.
Ah, thy cheek is cold and pale,
Soon thou'lt slumber in the vale,
Faded flowers shall strew thy grave,
Drooping willows o'er thee wave,
Autumn winds shall sing thy knell,
Gentle Summer, fare thee well!

# NIGHT STORMS.

To-night the rain is falling,
  The lightning blinds my eyes,
The clouds to earth are calling,
  The echoing earth replies.
I list with fearful wonder,
  As nigher still and nigher
The rattling, crashing thunder
  Bounds on its path of fire !
With every bound it maketh,
  With every flash of light,
My spirit backward taketh
  To other days its flight.
One year—alas, one only !
  It seems an age to me,
For I now sad and lonely,
  Was then so blest with thee.
One year ago the flashing
  Of light was in the sky,
The thunder wild and crashing,
  With stormy speed went by.
It echoed from the hill top,
  Its voice was in the vale,
And then as now each rain drop
  Was paired with one of hail.

The fierce north wind was rending
    The oaks so strong and tall,
Whose broken boughs descending
    Fell on our cabin wall.
Our lowly cabin trembled
    Beneath the rushing flood,
And I but half dissembled
    The fear that chilled my blood.
But thou wert then beside me,
    Thy arm was round me thrown,
And gently didst thou chide me
    For fears to thee unknown.
And while the storm was sweeping
    Adown the darkened sky,
And I in terror weeping
    Clung to thee tremblingly;
How fondly didst thou bless me,
    And smile my fears away,
And to thy bosom press me,
    And tell me of a day
When thou in early childhood,
    Beside thy native stream,
Didst wander in the wildwood,
    Beneath the sunset beam;
And how the sky was clouded
    With sudden storms that came
Like demon spirits shrouded
    In robes of living flame;
And how their voices sounded
    To thee, a fearless child,
As through the air they bounded,
    Like music strange and wild;

Like instruments from heaven,
   The drum and clarion shrill,
To every spirit given,
   And played on every hill.
The stormy chorus roaring
   Swept onward by the gale,
The rushing waters pouring
   Adown the darkened vale,
These sang to thy young spirit
   In glorious harmony,
For well didst thou inherit
   A passion for the free,
A passion for the fearless,
   With strength and beauty fraught;
And night storms wild and cheerless
   To thee no terror brought.
I felt my heart grow stronger
   By beating close to thine,
The lightning seemed no longer
   With angry glare to shine.
I blessed its light revealing
   To me thy tranquil eyes,
I blessed the thunder pealing
   In triumph through the skies.
I loved the storm for waking
   Such thoughts within thy breast,
My fetters too were breaking,
   My spirit too was blessed.
But now alone and tearful
   I list the tempest's roar,
My heart beats faint and fearful,
   I hear thy voice no more.

# THOU COMEST TO ME.

Thou comest when the midnight breeze
   All mournfully is sighing,
And but the dead leaves on the trees
   In broken tones replying —
Then comest thou to me;
Thy voice is like the night wind's voice,
   In mystery enshrouded:
Thy form is like my thought of thee
Where thou dost stand all gloriously
   In light and joy unclouded.
Thou dost enfold me as the breeze
Clasps in its viewless arms the trees,
   Whose thousand pulses tremble
If but the faintest breath they feel,
   Nor can their joy dissemble.

My heart is like the withered leaf,
   So faded, drooping, dying;
Yet one sweet joy it hath in grief
   To hear thy voice still sighing,
'O love, come up to me!
Come up to me!' O spirit voice,
   Mysterious in thy sweetness,

Fain would the withered leaf arise,
And to be near thee in the skies,
   Outstrip the wind in fleetness;
But while it waits a higher will,
Be thou amid the night wind still,
   And still for me be keeping,
As thou hast kept, though all unseen,
   Thy watch of love unsleeping.

6*

# AN APRIL DAY.

Fair children leave your careless play
    And bring your sweet wild flowers to me,
For all too sad my heart has grown
    To mingle in your revelry.
Come where the young spring sunlight falls
    So softly on this bank of green,
Where pale blue violets gem the grass
    Half hid beneath its emerald sheen.

Come pile your fragrant blossoms here,
    And here your own fair forms recline —
The good beside the beautiful;
    And while I thus your garlands twine,
I'll tell you why so strangely fell
    This sadness on my heart to day,
And why I sighed amid your mirth,
    And could not join your thoughtless play.

And yet, why should I speak my grief,
    Since hearts like yours, so light and young,
Have not the power of sympathy
    With those by deepest sorrow wrung.

Nay, Fanny, dry those violet eyes,
　　And check your sweet reproaches too;
But late you bade me spare a bud,
　　Nor from it brush the morning dew:

And shall I now the calyx break,
　　And rudely force a flower to bloom,
When well I know the passing cloud
　　Will shroud its tender heart with gloom?
Your heart is like that folded bud
　　So gently opening hour by hour,
A sudden storm might wake to life
　　A premature and drooping flower.

But seest thou down this grassy slope,
　　Yon rippling streamlet wind along,
And dost thou hear in murmurs sweet
　　Its low, but never-ceasing song?
I knew a stream far, far away,
　　As like to this as stream may be,
And sweeter blossoms gemmed its banks
　　Than these I twine for thee.

More sweet because beheld by one
　　Who ever wandered by my side,
And loved with me each flower that grew
　　Along that streamlet's sparkling tide.
O many an April day like this
　　We've roamed among those blooming trees,
The boxwood and the hawthorn fair,
　　Whose honeyed fragrance filled the breeze.

And still when comes the balmy spring,
   The scented hawthorn blooms as fair,
And year by year that nameless stream
   Will chant its own low music there.
But I shall wander there no more,
   Nor clasp that once beloved hand,
Cold, cold in dust it moulders now,
   And I am in a stranger's land.

This grassy bank, these budding trees,
   Familiar flowers and flowing stream,
With hallowed memories filled my heart,
   And made the past the present seem.
But when your cheerful laugh rang out,
   The charm was broke, the vision flown;
I saw you loving and beloved,
   I felt a stranger, and alone.

And this was why I turned aside
   And smiled not on your mirthful glee;
And this was why I could not bear
   To mingle in your revelry.
But now I see o'er each young face
   The light of purest friendship play,
So take the garlands I have twined,
   I'll make you sad no more to-day.

# MY MORNING DREAM.

I saw it in my morning dream —
 ᐧ A ship with all its sails outspread ;
Not on the sea, nor on the stream,
　But through the waveless air it sped. ᐧ

I saw it when with canvass white ᐧ
　Before the freshening breeze unrolled,
The unrisen sun's first beam of light
　Had tinged its sides with paly gold.

High up against the orient sky,
　Without a cloud its path to mar,
It held its way triumphantly,
　While o'er it beamed the morning star.

And still as swept the twilight sea
　That star-led ship so wondrous fair,
Sweet strains of angel minstrelsy
　Came floating backward on the air.

I could but weep, I could but gaze,
　And clasp my hands and wildly pray

That I might join their angel lays,
  And sing as fearlessly as they.

And lo, as still I prayed and wept,
  Still nearer to the earth they came;
And as the proud ship downward swept
  I heard them speak my humble name.

I heard one dear familiar tone —
  Familiar now, alas, no more;
One hand reached forth to clasp my own —
  A hand I oft had clasped before.

Without the power or wish to speak,
  I stood, with silent joy oppressed,
Till startled by my own wild shriek
  When struck the ship a rock's rude crest.

My prayers had lured it to my side
  While rung the angel anthem sweet,
And now it fell, in all its pride,
  A glorious ruin at my feet.

Forever stilled those triumph lays,
  That pilot star forever gone;
And I, alas, but weep and gaze
  Beside the ruined ship alone.

If this may be the doom of woe
  That waits my bark on being's stream,
I cannot tell; I only know
  I saw it in my morning dream.

# THE BLUEBIRD'S SONG.

Each morn beside my open door
  The blue bird sits and sings to me;
Those same sweet notes told o'er and o'er,
  But prove his loving constancy.
"I love thee;" thus the blue bird sings,
  And while the prelude swells more free,
He lightly lifts his azure wings,
  And turns his head to look at me.

I love thee! gently as the dew
  Upon the earth's green bosom falls,
So to my heart that love-note true
  A thought of former joy recalls.
I love thee! soft winds whisper love,
  Earth blooms amid its light divine,
It smiles from yon blue sky above,
  It warms thy heart and throbs in mine!

'Tis thus the blue bird sings to me,
  And thus he proves himself sincere,
By warbling o'er unceasingly
  Such notes as these where I can hear.

I love thee!   'Tis the sweetest song
  That ever bird or poet sung;
'Twill make the heart forget its wrong,
  E'en when by deepest sorrow wrung;

'Twill make the rose bloom on the cheek,
  The starlight brighten in the eyes;
No dearer words the lips can speak,
  No truer joy the heart can prize.
Sing on, sing on, thou darling bird,
  And say, I love thee, o'er and o'er,
But do not think I never heard
  That same sweet love song breathed before!

Once when a spring as bright as this
  Was blooming o'er the grassy lea,
The lips that pressed on mine a kiss
  Did softly whisper it to me.
And days and nights, for years and years,
  I've listened to that tender strain,
And still my heart unwearied hears
  The murmur of the sweet refrain.

I love thee; love, bend close to mine
  Thy loving eyes that say, I love,
Plain as the night stars say, we shine,
  · Without a word the lips to move.
And thus while mine are answering true,
  O love-bird by my open door,
Still flash in light thy wings of blue
  And sing, I love thee, evermore.

# ROSES BLOOM.

By the thorny wayside hedges,
Blushing o'er the rocky ledges,
Creeping 'mid the mossy sedges,
By the woodland streamlet's side,
    Roses bloom.
In the palace gardens glowing,
When the winds of June are blowing,
Or in darkened windows, knowing
Scarce the lamplight from the sun,
    Roses bloom.

When the summer sun declining
Slantly through the wood is shining,
Rustic lovers sweetly twining
Blossoms with their vows of love,
    Bless the Rose.
Through all life it shall remind them
Of the springtime left behind them,
Of the years that yet shall find them
Like the blended bloom and fragrance,
    Of the Rose.

Now the mother watch is keeping .
O'er her infant sweetly sleeping,
And with rapture almost weeping
As she sees on its fair cheek,
                    Roses bloom;
Then, while grief her heart is rending,
In her silent sorrow bending,
Tears are with the dewdrops blending,
On the Rose that blooms as fair
                    On its tomb.

Beneath the hedge the rose is dying,
From beauty's cheek the bloom is flying,
And youth and beauty lowly lying,
Leave the world they once have blessed
                    Wrapped in gloom.
But where they died new charms are springing;
As death its ceaseless change is bringing,
So life to life is ever clinging,
And still for life, for love and death,
                    Roses bloom.

# THE PINE.

As hour by hour at day's decline
I've sat and watched yon stately pine,
And seen its pencilled branches lie
So still against the wintry sky,
Or softly waving to and fro
To welcome down the falling snow,
I've wished that to my heart were given
The hopes that look alone to heaven;
Then, like the Pine tree ever green,
Amid the wintry tempests seen,
So calmly might I brave the strife,
And rise above the storms of life.
Then soft as on yon waving tree
Would fall the snows of age on me,
And birds that chant in early spring
Amid my sheltering boughs would sing;
And winds that through the forests moan,
Would sigh to me in gentler tone.
The soft, confiding whispering breeze
Would pass the leafless forest trees,

And welcomed to my thrilling breast,
Fold up its weary wings to rest.
So blessed and blessing might I rise
Calm and serenely toward the skies,
So might I be, at life's decline,
Loved as I love yon stately pine.

# "HATH NOT THY ROSE A CANKER?"

Pressed with the weight of morning dews
  Its slender stalk the rose was bending,
And red and white in changing hues
  Upon its cheek were sweetly blending.
     But underneath the leaflets bright,
     By blushing beauty hid from sight,
     Enamored with its fragrance rare,
     The canker worm was feasting there.

O thou who in thy youthful days
  Ambition's wreaths art proudly twining,
And fondly hoping worldly praise
  Will cheer thine after-years' declining,
     Beware lest every tempting rose
     That in ambition's pathway grows,
     Conceal beneath its semblance fair
     The lurking canker of despair.

And thou who in thine early morn
  For sin the paths of truth art leaving;

Remember, though no pointed thorn
  May pierce the garland thou art weaving,
      Yet every bud whence flowerets bloom
      Shall its own living sweets entomb,
      For deep the canker worm of care
      Is feasting on its vitals there.

Thou too, the beautiful and bright,
  At pleasure's shrine devoutly kneeling,
Dost thou not see the fatal blight
  Across thy roseate chaplet stealing?
      Time hath not touched with fingers cold
      Those glossy leaves of beauty's mould,
      And yet each bud and blossom gay
      Is marked for slow but sure decay

O ye who sigh for flowers that bloom
  In one eternal spring of gladness,
Where beauty finds no darkened tomb,
  And joy hath never dreamed of sadness,
      There is a realm ye all may know,
      Where Sharon's fadeless roses blow;
      Nor blighting breath of sin or care,
      Nor sorrow's canker enter there!

# APRIL AND MAY.

The changing April sunlight played
   Its merry gambols on the stream,
Now veiling all its waves in shade,
   Then glancing forth with dazzling gleam;
Now touching with a softer light
   The mimic whirlpools on its breast,
Then gilding with a radiance bright
   Each tiny wavelet's lifted crest.
The flowers that grew by thousands there
   In many a careless tangled braid,
Gave fragrance to the restless air
   That 'mid their bright corollas played.
The scented boxwood by the hill
   Was holding all its blossoms up,
And April raindrops sparkled still
   In each uplifted, snowy cup.
Beside the stream the snow white thorn
   Spread out its virgin blossoms fair,
And incense with the blossoms born
   Went floating through the sunlit air.

The long grass waved its emerald plumes
　　Unceasing in the western breeze,
And birds that breathed the sweet perfumes
　　Were warbling 'midst the budding trees.

Sweet morn, the last of April days,
　　'Twas meet that one so fair as thou,
Should fade before our longing gaze,
　　With garlands blooming on thy brow.
'Twas meet that o'er thy infant bloom
　　The softest breath of spring should blow;
Twas meet that round thy early tomb
　　The fairest flowers of spring should grow.
For ere another morn may break
　　In radiant beauty o'er the earth,
The sweetly blushing May shall wake
　　To light and life, to joy and mirth.
And all the dew that nature showers
　　Like gems along thy pathway now,
Is but to nourish brighter flowers
　　To twine around her cherub brow.
And birds with practiced notes must sing
　　Their sweetest anthems on the breeze,
'Tis meet the favorite child of Spring
　　Be met with honors such as these.

And thus was born the beauteous May,
Amid the dew, amid the bloom,
　　She rose, like beauty from decay,
To strew fresh buds o'er April's tomb.

# A SONG FOR MAY.

While the fresh green grass is springing,
   Starred and gemmed with countless flowers,
And the sweet young May is bringing
   Perfume from her far off bowers,
While the robin's song is ringing
   Through the balmy morning hours,
Every poet too is singing —
   Singing of the sweet May showers,
Singing of the dawning beauty,
   Of this lovely world of ours!

Hark! the blue bird's song entrancing
   From the budding orchard rings,
While the rosy light is glancing
   From his restless azure wings!
Poets, while the spring advancing
   Thus her cheering music brings,
O remember that to mortals
   Ye are birds without their wings!
Poet-birds, and bird-like poets,
   Each is happiest while he sings.

7

Then together join in chorus,
    Welcome in the smiling May;
Bless the green buds bending o'er us,
    They'll be leaves another day.
Bless the wind that goes before us,
    Waking beauty in our way,
Till we dream it doth restore us
    Back to life's sweet April day!
Birds and poets join in chorus,
    Hail the birth of blooming May!

# OUR WILDWOOD HOME.

A lowly wildwood home is ours,
No spacious halls, no lofty towers,
No gardens gay with fairy bowers,
    Nor pomp nor pride are here.
Yet wealth with fingers nerved with gold,
Those magic fingers bright and cold,
Amid the realms of romance old
    Ne'er wrought a home so dear.

Its summer roof is gay with moss,
And climbing vines and roses cross,
And blooming trees their branches toss
    In breeze and sunshine there;
And when her garland autumn weaves
Of coral seeds and painted leaves,
The moss grows gray along the eaves,
    Like age's whitening hair,

When piled with winter's drifting snow,
Though fierce the north winds round it blow,

No chill can reach the hearth below
   Where social love holds sway,
Where cheerily each winter night,
While blazing fires burn high and bright,
The scattered household band unite
   Around the hearthstone gray.

The dear old hearthstone of our home!
Where'er on earth our steps shall roam,
No purer light than thine can come,
   Life's pilgrimage to cheer —
Light from the blazing brands piled high,
And holier light, that cannot die,
From each warm lip and loving eye
   That makes our household dear.

# LONG AGO.

Long ago when I a dreamer
  By the April brooks went straying,
I but saw the opening blossoms,
  I but heard the breezes playing.
Pressing oft the springing mosses
  Where had slept the winter snow,
I could feel no thorns beneath them,
  In that blissful long ago.

Long ago when half awakened
  From that idle springtime dreaming,
I but saw the summer splendor
  O'er life's sparkling waters beaming.
Twining then hope's fairy garlands,
  Roseate in their summer glow,
Could I think of blight or darkness,
  In that radiant long ago?

Long ago all dreaming vanished,
  Died the springtime blossoms tender,
Long ago the autumn shadows
  Fell upon that summer splendor!
I with weary hands am toiling
  Where life's darkened stream moves slow,
And like withered leaves around me,
  Lie the hopes of long ago.

# MY PRISONED BIRD.

I listen to each bird that sings
　　Among these budding trees of May,
And weep for one whose weary wings
　　Are folded in its cage to-day.
A dreamy, drooping, silent bird,
　　Nor note of joy nor plaint of woe
Are from its lonely prison heard —
　　Ah me, it was not always so!

Poor bird! my pet, my idol too,
　　In those bright years when life was joy;
When 'mid the flowers in May's sweet dew
　　Thou saug'st of bliss without alloy!
Of bliss that would be thine and mine
　　Beyond those far unfolding gates,
Where by her radiant noonday shrine
　　The ever-glorious Future waits.

Ah me; how wild the pathway grew
　　As toward life's noontide gates we came!

MY PRISONED BIRD. 151

Hot winds drank up the sweet May dew,
  And crisped the flowers as with a flame.
Strange murmurs in the air were heard,
  Of toil and strife and wild unrest;
Strange voices mocked my timid bird,
  And drove it shrinking to my breast.

I clasped it, trembling, shrinking too ;
  Yet onward urged by life's rude throng,
I did what strong ones bade me do,
  And stilled for aye its voice of song.
I closed it in my darkened heart,
  Shut out the light of love's sweet day,
·And there it sadly droops apart,
  Uncheered by all this bloom of May.

# THE WHIP-POOR-WILL.

In dimness of twilight, all sadly and lonely,
  A youthful adventurer rode o'er the plain,
The stillness was broke by the whippoorwill only,
  As sadly he sounded his mournful refrain.
      By the stream near the mill
      Sang the lone whippoorwill,
And echo far distant caught up the wild strain,
      Whip-poor-will, whip-poor-will;
She murmured it o'er to her favorite hill,
  And faintly the hill sung it back to the plain.

The wanderer sighed, for his steps were departing
  Far, far from his home and the land of his birth,
And, spite of his pride, the warm tear drops were
    starting,
    Unchecked and unheeded they fell to the earth,
      While unceasingly still
      Sang the lone whippoorwill,
And sadly re-echoed the mournful refrain
      Whip-poor-will, whip-poor-will;
But fainter it grew as he paused on the hill,
  And turned his last look toward the valley and
    plain.

Then he thought of his parents who gave him their
　　blessing,
　Of sisters who murmured their tearful adieu,
Of brothers whose hands he no more should be press-
　　ing,
　　But most of a maiden whose soft eyes of blue
　　　　Seemed to follow him still,
　　　　While the lone whippoorwill
More sadly was sounding the mournful refrain,
　　　　Whip-poor-will, whip-poor-will;
Till the wanderer turned with a sigh from the hill
　And the shadows of night settled over the plain.

Now years have gone by, and the youth is a stranger,
　Still far from his kindred and far from his love,
But there lies near his heart through all peril and
　　danger
　　A soft golden ringlet encircling a dove;
　　　　It was there on the hill
　　　　When the lone whippoorwill
So mournfully sounded the solemn refrain,
　　　　Whip-poor-will, whip-poor-will;
'Tis the charm of his life, and he'll cherish it still,
　As the gift of the maiden who dwelt on the plain.

He wanders alone, in the twilight, in sadness,
　He dreams of the maiden, the ringlet, the dove,
When sudden his eyes are uplifted in gladness,
　　The night birds are wheeling in circles above!
　　　　Never, since by the mill
　　　　When the lone whippoorwill
So sadly was sounding the mournful refrain,
　　　　Whip-poor-will, whip-poor-will,

Hath he heard the wild notes that his bosom could
    thrill,
And now he could weep but to hear them again.

But in vain may he linger, in vain may he listen,
    The night-birds like arrows shoot over the plain —
They are gone, and the cold stars in mockery glisten,
    While silence and darkness close round him again.
        Nevermore by the mill
        Shall the lone whippoorwill
For him be repeating the mournful refrain,
        Whip-poor-will, whip-poor-will;
He knows the dark omen can bode him but ill,
    The maid is another's — his worship is vain!

# MY BOYHOOD'S LOVE.

My boyhood's love! The old man sighed
   And shook his thin locks in the breeze,
No words in all the world beside
   Can thrill my aged heart like these.

My life seems like yon wintry cloud
   Slow moving down the evening sky,
From its high station, cold and proud,
   It darkly sinks, alone to die.

Alone, but for the one bright star
   That far beyond it beams in heaven;
Alone, but for such joys as are
   From angel minds to mortals given!

O can it be that she who died
   With youth's bright roses on her brow,
Who slept to wake in beauty's pride
   Will stoop to know and love me now?

What dark, mysterious fate is this
    That bids the weary still live on,
Till the last drop of wretchedness
    From life's embittered cup is gone?

Look on this frail, decaying form,
    These sightless eyes, these locks of snow,
This pulse that once beat high and warm,
    Scarce bids the vital current flow.

Yet sure as in its beauty fair
    Beyond the cloud the star beams true,
So sure my boyhood's love is there,
    So sure she knows and loves me too!

Ask not her name: the angels know
    What name her spirit bears above,
The only one she has below
    Is in my heart — my boyhood's love!

# "LIFE IS REAL."

"Life is real! Life is earnest!"
  Why that sigh?
Why that look of hopeless sorrow
When thou thinkest of the morrow?
  Why that tearful eye?
Bind again thy loosened tresses,
And unclasp the hand that presses
  Thy cold brow;
"Life is real! Life is earnest!"
Vainly to the past thou turnest,
  That shall fail thee now.

'Tis but labor that awaits thee
  On the morn;
Other hands have wrought before thee,
Other eyes are watching o'er thee,
  Though from kindred torn.
Shall thy spirit droop and languish,
And these burning tears of anguish
  Pale thy cheek,
While thy woman heart is fearing
Lest the world thy sighs o'erhearing,
  Now should call thee weak?

Tears from thee are like the life drops
  From the vine;
Let thine eyes their lustre keeping
Save the strength thus lost in weeping,

Why shouldst thou repine,
While the promise still is given —
"Weary hearts find rest in heaven!"
Look above :
There's one truth that cannot alter,
Earthly friends may fail and falter,
God is always love.

O 'tis not the far off future,
          Ever bright
With fair hopes around it springing,
That from thy lone heart is wringing
          These sad drops to-night.
'Tis the living present, lonely,
'Tis the day of trial, only
          Dreaded now,
For thy strength will come to-morrow,
And thou'lt look on care and sorrow
          With unclouded brow.

"Life is real !   Life is earnest !"
          God of Heaven!
What alternate pride and meekness,
Giant strength and infant weakness
          To the heart are given !
Worn with grief and gay with gladness,
Crowned with reason, dark with madness,
          Must it be,
Ere its pilgrimage is ended,
Ere its dust with dust is blended,
          And its life with thee !

# THE SPIRIT'S WARNING.

Every night a spirit cometh
  And it whispereth unto me —
Dream'st thou yet, O slumbering mortal,
  Wake and grasp reality!
Dreams are for the child of fancy,
  Visions haunt the idle brain;
All thy youth has passed in dreaming,
  Canst thou call it back again?
Think on what thy heart once promised
  In its deep unspoken vow,
See that promise unfulfilled,
  Waken and redeem it now!

Thus to me a spirit whispereth
  In the silent hours of sleep,
And my heart, awaking, pondereth
  O'er its warning sad and deep.
Since my childhood's twilight morning
  I have thought what life might be,
When the noon of womanhood
  Threw its hallowed light on me.

In those dim and early moments,
  Viewed through fancy's light alone,
Who could paint the wondrous glory
  That around the future shone?
All that claims the artist's pencil
  In the dew-enameled flowers,
All that poets dream of beauty
  Born amid hope's radiant bowers,
All that science hath of brightness
  Circling round her earthly name,
All the splendor that she borrows  ·
  From religion's purer flame,
All of joy that love hath promised
  ·  To the young heart's fondest prayer,
Life's sweet hopes and dreams of heaven,
  Gathered in one halo there!
Then from out that dazzling future,
  Came a voice whose solemn tone
Trembling o'er my heart's deep pulses
  Woke an echo in my own.
Lo, all prophet-like and holy
  Rose the solemn voice of Truth,
O'er the light, beguiling numbers
  Hope was chanting to my youth.
And it told me life was changeful
  As the wind-tossed ocean wave,
Where each crested billow sinking
  Brings another to its grave.
And it spoke in accents mournful
  Of life's joys by sorrow crossed,
Of its own high shrine forsaken,
  And the soul's fair Eden lost.

Knelt I then, subdued and prayerful,
　Faded fancy's light away,
And o'er all the distant future
　Shone a milder, purer ray.
With a purpose deep and earnest
　Bent I at Truth's holy shrine,
Vowing from my inmost spirit
　But to heed its voice divine.
Through my life that vow hath ever
　Prompted each new lay I sung;
But too oft a trifling semblance
　Fancy's pencil o'er them flung.
Like the half awakened sleeper
　Clinging to his morning dreams,
Blending still the shades of darkness
　With the light that round him beams;
Dreaming though the day be breaking,
　Idly pleased with each new ray,
Hailing, but with languid pleasure,
　Tokens of a brighter day, —
Thus my youth has passed in dreaming,
　Now a spirit saith to me ; —
"Dream no more, O slumbering mortal !
　Wake and grasp reality.
Lo, the light of Truth is round thee,
　Hail it for the joy divine
It hath brought to other spirits,
　Though it brings not peace to thine.
Though the charm of life be broken
　Like the foam on ocean's wave,
Where each crested billow sinking
　Brings another to its grave,

Still with higher hopes and purer
    Than beguiled thy aimless youth,
Let thy songs henceforth be given
    For the earnest, living truth!"

# MY HEART GROWS SAD FOR THEE.

My heart grows sad for thee, my love,
   When in thy gentle eyes
For my o'erburdened life so oft
   The tears of pity rise.

When sympathetic weariness
   On thy dear brow I see,
I wish that I might build a bower
   Like Rosamond's for thee;

A bower secure from every ill
   That human heart hath wrung,
Where thou might'st dwell without a care
   Thy sister flowers among.

And I, who may not, dare not shrink
   Life's wildest storm to meet,
Might sometimes come to breathe a word
   Of worship at thy feet;

Might know that all the joy of love,
　And life's sweet hopes were thine,
Though ever to my lips were pressed
　Its mingled gall and wine.

Thou tremblest in my arms beloved,
　Thy tears are falling free, —
Ah, would that life had more of light
　And less of gloom for thee!

Yet by these clinging arms I know,
　And by thy pleading eyes,
Thou still would'st pray to share my lot
　Though darker tempests rise.

Thou would'st not give one hour of bliss
　Our suffering love hath known,
To sit in regal pomp beside
　A monarch on his throne!

Forgive the thought, though born of love,
　That would have robbed thy life
Of joy that they alone can feel
　Who share its fiercest strife.

Thou gavest but the sympathy
　To thy sweet nature true; —
When bends the oak beneath the blast
　The vine must tremble too.

Then closer clasp thy twining arms
　Till strife and storm are o'er,

I will not tear thee from my side
  While thus the tempests roar.

Misfortunes cloud our life's young morn,
  The skies are dark above,
But side by side we'll brave the storm,
  Our strength our steadfast love.

# POESY.

" Thou art a rock,
I, a weak wave, would break on thee and die."

*Alex. Smith.*

O not a rock, sweet Poesy, art thou to me,
    Where thousand stronger waves than I might fall
From thy cold front to that unpitying sea
    That opes to shroud them in oblivion's pall;
Where for one wave that might its foam wreaths
        bear
    To thy stern brow in mockery o'er them bending,
A thousand should sink down in weak despair,
    Their love for thee with their own death notes
        blending;
For man would love, and woman worship thee,
Though thou wert rock, and they but ripples on the
        sea.

O not a rock to me, sweet Poesy, art thou,
    Where braver barks than mine, with drooping
        sail,
Lost helm, and shivered mast, and broken prow,
    Might sink beside thee in the billows pale;

Where for one bark whose daring helmsman might
  In life's last flow on thy cold breast be lying,
A thousand wrecks would strew the waves of night,
  And love for thee still crown the woe of dying!
For man would love and woman worship thee,
If thou wert rock, and they but frail barks on the
      sea.


O not a rock, earth-worshiped Poesy; thou art
  Life's blossom-crowned and balmy breathing spring,
A fount of joy perennial in the world's great heart,
  A bird whose song at rest or on the wing
Is ever sweet; the bright electric flame
  That fills all nature with a life immortal,
Our angel part, the inheritance that came
  From heaven, and goes before us to heaven's por-
      tal!
Man well may love, and woman worship thee,
Thou star-eyed child of light, undying Poesy!


O not a rock art thou to whom my panting soul
  Instinctive flies in all its joy or woe!
Thou whose sweet voice the storms of passion can
      control,
  And change wild griefs to music's softest flow!
Thou on whose breast of tenderest sympathy
  I still recline with confidence unfearing,
While the same smile in childhood bent on me,
  Beams o'er me yet, more radiantly, more cheering.
O thus forever may I cling to thee,
My destiny's one hope— my heart's one idol, Poesy!

8

# MARCH!

The march of the seasons through sunshine and rain
Has brought the bleak March to our hearthstones
    again;
  His winds piping shrill,
  Over valley and hill,
    Give a watchword of duty to all;
  To each lip the word springs,
  But most cheerily rings,
    In the morn at the farmer's loud call,
                      March!

Come boys, to the barnyard, your cattle to feed,
And girls of your cows and your poultry take heed,
  Though the morning is chill,
  And the March winds blow shrill,
    Come cheerfully forth at the call;
  There is life on the wings
  Of the gale as it sings
    In the pride of its freedom to all,
                      March !

Come men, with your axes and sinews of strength,
The trees in yon fallow must measure their length
    On the ground 'neath the hill,
    Where the wind whistles shrill,
      Ere the shadows of evening shall fall ;
  Let our sturdy strokes ring
  A glad welcome to spring,
    Keeping time to her life-giving call,
                  March !

We'll see to our fences, our harrows and plows,
We'll give extra care to our lambkins and cows;
    That when March winds are still,
    And o'er valley and hill
      The warm sunlight of April shall fall,
  No hindrance they'll bring
  To the labors of spring,
    While I forth at the head of you all,
                  March !

We'll march in the furrows so deep and so true,
And plant the bright corn where the dark forest
    grew ;
    Our rich fallows we'll till,
    And as hopefully still
      From our hands shall the golden grains fall,
  Of the harvest we'll sing —
  'Tis the promise of Spring
    To all farmers who now heed her call ;
                  March !

8

And thus through all seasons, in sunshine and rain,
Till March shall come round to our hearthstones
  again,
  With a steady good will,
  We will sow, reap and till,
   And, still mindful of life's coming fall,
  We can joyfully sing
  When our ripe sheaves we bring
   At the sound of our Maker's last call,
        March !

# A SPRING SONG.

The days are lengthening on the earth,
　And deepening in the azure heaven ; —
How thankfully our hearts look up
　To Him who hath the Spring-time given.
Not one of all the seasons four,
　Though rich in bloom and bounteousness,
Brings to our life such tender joy,
　So sweet a crown of hope as this.

We take the Summer's harvest gifts,
　And turn, with heat and toil oppressed,
To lay the burdens that we bear
　On placid Autumn's matron breast.
Then, shrinking from her fading charms,
　We welcome Winter's icy reign,
Well conscious that his parting breath
　Will wake the sweet young Spring again.

Young, with that pure, immortal life
　Born at the threshold of the tomb,
And sweet with all its prophet buds
　Full of the Summer's ripened bloom.
O God, though from our life Thou take
　The dearest treasures time can bring,
Blight not the tender joys that wake
　Perennial with each blooming Spring !

# HOEING CORN.

Out in the earliest light of morn
Ralph was hoeing the springing corn;
The dew fell flashing from blades of green
Wherever his glancing hoe was seen,
While dark and mellow the hard earth grew
Beneath his strokes so strong and true.
   And steadily still, hill after hill,
As the sun went up he swung his hoe,
    Hoe, hoe, hoe, — row after row;
From the earliest light of the summer morn,
Till the noonday sound of the dinner horn.

What was Ralph thinking of all the morn,
Out in the summer heat hoeing corn,
With the sweat and dust on his hands and face,
And toiling along at that steady pace ?
A clear light beamed in his eye the while,
And round his lips was a happy smile,
   As steadily still, hill after hill,
While the sun went down he swung his hoe;
    Hoe, hoe, hoe — row after row,
Faster toward nightfall than even at morn
He hastened his steps through the springing corn.

Across the road from this field of corn
Was the stately home where Ralph was born;
Where his father counted his stores of gold,
And his lady mother so proud and cold
Lived but for the silks and gauze and lace
That shrouded her faded form and face;
　While steadily still, hill after hill,
Unthought of went Ralph, and swung his hoe,
　Hoe, hoe, hoe — row after row,
Day after day through the springing corn,
Toward the humble home of Isabel Lorn.


This he was thinking of all the morn,
And all day long as he hoed the corn, —
"How sweet 'twill be when the shadows fall
Over that little brown cottage wall,
To sit by its door 'neath the clustering vine,
With Isabel's dear little hand in mine!
　So cheerily still, hill after hill,
From morning till night I'll swing my hoe,
　Hoe, hoe, hoe — row after row,
Knowing each step through the springing corn,
Is bringing me nearer to Isabel Lorn!"


O glad was he then when the growing corn
Shielded his steps from his mother's scorn:
And glad that his father's miser hand
Had barred all help from his fertile land;
So safely he kept his forest flower,
And dreamed of her beauty hour by hour,
　As steadily still, hill after hill,

Through the field so broad he swung his hoe,
   Hoe, hoe, hoe — row after row,
Knowing each step through the growing corn
Was bringing him nearer to Isabel Lorn.

So months passed on, and the ripened corn
Was laid on the ground one autumn morn,
While under the sod in the churchyard blest
Are two low graves where the aged rest.
The father has left broad lands and gold,
And the mother her wealth of silks untold;
   And sweet Isabel — why need I tell
What she said to Ralph when without his hoe
   He sought her side ?   It was not " no "
That made her the mistress one summer morn,
Of that stately home by the field of corn.

# KING AND QUEEN.

I am a king in my own domain,
    And my little wife is queen,
And jointly over our realm we reign,
    A royal couple I ween.

Beauty and grace are the robes that flow
    From her lily shoulders down,
The gems of truth on her bosom glow,
    And love is her golden crown.

But her dainty hands are brown with toil,
    Her cheeks with the breezes' kiss,
And she works for a tiller of the soil
    As if work for him were bliss.

I am the king and the tiller too,
    My farm is my proud domain,
And the will to dare and the strength to do
    Are the sceptres of my reign.

ε*

At my touch the teeming earth yields up
Her wealth for my feast and store;
The nectar of health brims high my cup,
My measure of bliss runs o'er.

O ne'er was a happier realm I ween
Than ours 'neath the arching sky,
And never a happier king and queen
Than my little wife and I!

# SIGNS OF SPRING.

## TO MARY IN THE COUNTRY.

You wonder how we city folks
    Can know that it is Spring,
With no green grass beneath our feet,
    No wildwood birds to sing !
With no sweet blossoms springing up
    To brighten all the way,
You wonder how we ever came
    To know that it was May.
You say the fragrant pastures now,
    Where golden cowslips grow,
Are filled with calves and little lambs,
    That run and gambol so !
And o'er the furrows black and long,
    Like emeralds clasped in jet,
Each holding in its folded heart
    A sparkling diamond set,
The tender corn is peeping out,
    Unfolding one by one

The dainty leaves that soon will flaunt
　　More broadly in the sun.
You say that o'er the waving wheat,
　　Through all the breezy day,
Like fairy children at their sport
　　The lights and shadows play;
And that the blooming orchard trees
　　Their branching censers swing,
Perfuming all the sunlit air,
　　And thus *you* know 'tis Spring !
But wonder how we city folks,
　　Without the wild bird's tune,
Or lambs and orchards, wheat and corn,
　　Can tell when it is June !

Dear Mary, what a simple girl !
　　How very countrified !
Your ignorance of city life
　　Is shocking to my pride !
You seem to think that nothing green
　　Can grow and flourish here ;
Why, greenness is the very thing
　　For which we're noted, dear.
Whichever way you go, across,
　　Or up, or down the street,
You're pretty sure some specimens
　　Of that bright hue to meet.
And if you knew our business ways,
　　You'd soon begin to see
The greenest of your grass is pale
　　Beside our verdancy.

Unlike you simple country folks,
  Who in your plodding way
Will "trade" and "dicker," "swap" and "sell,"
  And always get your pay,
Our city dealers sell "on time,"
  They pile the profits high,
In hopes to make a double haul
  When needed, by and by.
They're green enough to stretch their hands,
  Expectant, for the gold,
But soon discover 'tis themselves,
  And not the goods, are "sold."
And editors will trust their friends
  Their paper bills for years,
Though warned by starving publishers
  They sow to reap in tears.
O never in your greenest woods
  Where rankest verdure is,
Could verdant hunters come across
  A greener thing than this!
And when their duns come back endorsed,
  "Poor," "Dead," or "Ran away,"
I do not think your silly lambs
  More sheepish feel than they!
No; greeneys are not wanting here,
  And through our city roam
Calves quite as big as any two
  Around your country home.

You talk of growing wheat and corn
  And orchards blooming gay,—

But we had plainer signs than these
  To tell us it was May.
Soon as the snow had left our streets,
  And dust had come instead,
Each lady took a little sign
  And tied it on her head.
But fearing these might not be seen,
  Because they were so small,
Each had upon her shoulders hung
  A rainbow-colored shawl;
And then with costly 'broideries
  O'er hoops of monstrous size,
Or balmorals whose dazzling hues
  Might almost blind your eyes,
O'erspread with skirts of trailing length
  From fashions o'er the seas,
They launched upon the avenue,
  And sailed before the breeze.
By skirt and shawl and top-knot gay,
  And ribbons fluttering,
Whene'er we looked upon the street
  We knew that it was Spring.
There roses stalked in stately pride
  With flaunting lily-belles,
As if in sportive strife to see
  Who'd make the biggest swells!
And dandy-lions, neat and trim,
  Enlivened all the scene,
With ornaments of yellow hue
  Well set on *living green!*

So, Mary, by these signs you see,
  Though from your woods away,
We needed not your grass and flowers
  To tell us it was May.
And thus, without your sunlit dells,
  Or wild bird's simple tune,
No doubt our rose-and-lily-belles
  Will tell us when 'tis June.

# THE SNOW.

The snow is coming, the beautiful snow!
  How fast through the air it is flying;
Like Charity's mantle it covers from sight
The ruin that Autumn had made in his might,
When he ravished the blossoms so lovely and
    bright.
  And left them all withered and dying.
The snow covers all, the beautiful snow;
The springtime is gone, and the summer's bright
    glow,
And no longer with well-feigned accents of woe
  The hypocrite Autumn is sighing.

The snow, the glittering snow has come!
  From morn till night the bells are ringing;
A livelier welcome was never heard
From the throat of a gay and gladsome bird,
When he saw by a leaf the wind had stirred,
  The first young violet springing.
The snow bird too with the snow has come —
O Willie, throw down your noisy drum,
And bring to this dear little warbler a crumb,
  For which he will pay you in singing.

O rosy-cheeked and laughing girls,
  For your delight the snow comes down;
It melts amid your shining curls,
  Your raven braids and tresses brown.
Swift through the air the rounded ball
  By roguish boys is deftly thrown;
No matter which shall break its fall,
  Your head, or Fanny's, or my own!
Scarce whiter than your neck it fell,
  Like snow on snow bank lightly —
Another backward flies — that's well!
  No other hand could throw so sprightly!
O merrily then, fair children, sing,
Not for the languishing, balmy Spring,
Not for the Summer or Autumn — no,
Sing for the snow, the beautiful snow!

# THE CLOSING YEAR.

The year is dying with the day,
And blending with the twilight gray
    The shadows come and go;
With noiseless step across the floor,
And dusky banners waving o'er,
    I see them moving slow.

The twilight deepens into gloom,
And darkly round my silent room
    The phantom hopes arise —
Such haunting shapes as once had form
Of life and beauty glowing warm,
    Beneath more smiling skies.

I see them oft at hours like this,
When lingering daylight waits to kiss
    The blushing star of eve,
Then slowly pales his love-lit fires,
And down the crimson sky retires,
    As loth that star to leave.

And oft I wake to hear their call
When midnight drops her sombre pall
    Adown yon arch of blue ;
And I those shadowy bands among,
Have still their mournful marches sung
    Till I am mournful too.

But vain to-night shall be their charms,
Their beckoning hands and twining arms:
    Come hither Adelaide :
Now place thy fair young cheek to mine,
And let thy arms around me twine,
    Nor tremble 'mid this shade.

Upon thy breast no weary years
In sorrow born, baptised in tears,
    With life's sweet hopes have died ;
But lovely in thy·youthful morn,
An opening rose without a thorn,
    Thou standest by my side.

Thy trusting, hopeful smiles dispel
The glooms that o'er my spirit fell ;
    The haunting shadows flee,
And standing by thy side I seem
As walking in a blissful dream,
    A hopeful child like thee.

But ah, to-morrow's light will bring
Another leaf to crown thy spring ;

For me, perchance a tear ;
Yet in my dream methinks I see
A brighter day of hope for me
Is dawning with the year.

# A SONG FOR NEW YEAR'S EVE.

Away with thoughts of pall and bier,
And cypress bough and funeral tear,
And wailings for the dying year.
Our household fires shall burn to-night
With warmer glow, while children bright
Dance round us in the rosy light.

Life was not given for tears and groans,
The god-like gift of speech for moans,
Or faces made for churchyard stones.
Hang the green holly on your walls,
And let the children's laughing calls
Re-echo through the lighted halls.

Those who have killed the year may weep,
And low in dust and ashes creep,
With wild laments and anguish deep;
But we who loved him best while here,
Can bid him go with festal cheer,
And lights and garlands round his bier.

He came to us a helpless child,
Amid the snows of winter wild —
Our hearths with blazing logs we piled,
We gave him shelter from the storm,
And closely wrapped his shivering form,
In softest wools and ermine warm.

We fed him from our garden store —
The richest fruits our orchards bore,
·And nuts from many a foreign shore.
Our corn and wine his strength supplied,
Till, grown to boyhood by our side,
We gloried in his youthful pride.

We gave him flocks and fertile lands,
We bowed our heads to his commands,
And tilled his fields with willing hands;
When lo, to crown his manhood's morn,
The ripening wheat, and tasseled corn,
Were of our loving labor born.

Through all the summer's noontide heat,
We toiled amid the clover sweet,
And piled its fragrance at his feet.
We reaped his fields of waving grain,
Then plowed o'er all the vale and plain,
And sowed the hopeful seed again,

And when the autumn's withered leaves
Fell rustling round our household eaves,
We gathered in his golden sheaves,

We bound his furrowed brow with maize,
And honored his declining days
With jubilees of grateful praise.

His work is done ; his Harvest-home
Is gathered where no blight can come,
And his sealed lips are sweetly dumb
From the full perfectness of bliss,
The rapture trance that ever is
Just where the Heavenly life meets this.

We want for him no death bells slow,
No sable plumes and hearse of woe,
With mourners wailing as they go.
But bring, in place of tolling knells,
The music of your merry bells,
And cheerful songs for sad farewells.

Hang the green holly on the walls,
Let social mirth and music calls
Ring through your festal lighted halls.
Life from the Old Year's death is born,
Let bright'ning hopes with smiles adorn
The breaking of the New Year's Morn !

Lily of the Lesbian Isle,
   Twin in heart with Lesbos' Rose,
O'er thy life's too fleeting smile,
   O'er thy early ended woes,
   Fond Romance a glory throws.

Pallid as thine emblem flower,
   In thy humble garb arrayed,
At the distaff hour by hour,
   Through all change of sun and shade,
   Sitt'st and sing'st thou, Lesbian maid.

Weary grow the fingers slight,
   Still the wheel with ceaseless turn
Weds the morning to the night,
   Heedless as thy parent stern
   Of the thoughts that in thee burn.

Endless through the hands so small
   Glides the thread for Lesbos' looms;
Spinning thus thy young life's pall,
   O'er thy spirit fall no glooms
   And thy soul in beauty blooms.

Patient at the distaff bent
  To thine ear a murmur comes,
Message sweet by nature sent —
    By each bird and bee that hums
    Through her forests dropping gums;

By each wandering wind that blows
  O'er the loved Ægean waves;
By each mountain stream that flows
    From the naiad haunted caves
    Where the lonely cistus waves,

Down the green hills, orange crowned,
  O'er the sunbright slopes that lie
Garlanded by vines around
    Where the purple clusters vie
    With the purple Lesbian sky.

Soft the tender floods of song
  Borne by winds and waves and streams —
Lethe for the spirit's wrong —
    Pour their splendors through thy dreams
    Till an eden round thee beams.

There impassioned, bold and strong,
  Sappho o'er her golden lyre,
Rose of beauty, love and song,
    Blushing breathes the fond desire
    That consumes her heart of fire.

Thou, Erinna, listening all,
  Thrilling, trembling in the glow
Of the love-born airs that fall

On thè winds that come and go
Through thy casement dark and low,

Thou, the Lesbian Lily fair,
 O'er thy distaff drooping cold,
Type of genius bound by care,
 Speakest through the legend old
 To these years of sterner mould.

Music-sweet the murmurs come
 Where thy toilworn sisters kneel,
Wearied with the ceaseless hum
 Of life's ever turning wheel,
 Wounded by the distaff's steel.

Toiling hands that may not rest,
 Hearts the world may ne'er beguile,
Lips that love hath never pressed,
 Bless thy hopeful song and smile
 Lily of the Lesbian Isle!

www.ingramcontent.com/pod-product-compliance
Lightning Source LLC
Chambersburg PA
CBHW030842270326
41928CB00007B/1182